LAWS AND LEGISLATION

# JURISDICTION

## SELECT ANALYSES, CONSIDERATIONS AND CASES

# LAWS AND LEGISLATION

Additional books in this series can be found on Nova's website under the Series tab.

Additional E-books in this series can be found on Nova's website under the E-book tab.

# CRIMINAL JUSTICE, LAW ENFORCEMENT AND CORRECTIONS

Additional books in this series can be found on Nova's website under the Series tab.

Additional E-books in this series can be found on Nova's website under the E-book tab.

LAWS AND LEGISLATION

# JURISDICTION

## SELECT ANALYSES, CONSIDERATIONS AND CASES

AUDREY E. STEWART
AND
DERECK A. WASHINGTON
EDITORS

Nova Science Publishers, Inc.
*New York*

For permission to use material from this book please contact us:
Telephone 631-231-7269; Fax 631-231-8175
Web Site: http://www.novapublishers.com



**LIBRARY OF CONGRESS CATALOGING-IN-PUBLICATION DATA**

ISBN: 978-1-62081-429-1

*Published by Nova Science Publishers, Inc. † New York*

# CONTENTS

# PREFACE

In the realm of jurisprudence, the issue of jurisdiction can be quite complicated. The select analyses provided in this book examine some of the myriad elements and considerations that arise in matters of jurisdiction. Included are: an overview of Congress's ability to participate in litigation before Article III courts; the interplay of borders, turf, cyberspace and jurisdiction; Indian tribal civil jurisdiction's reach over non-Indians; Supreme Court appellate jurisdiction over military court cases; federal jurisdiction in copyright registration; and challenges to "large" orders under federal contracts.

Chapter 1 - As disputes between Congress and the executive become more prevalent, questions about Congress's ability to turn to the federal courts for vindication of its powers and prerogatives, or for declarations that the executive is in violation of the law or the Constitution, begin to arise. This report seeks to provide an overview of Congress's ability to participate in litigation before Article III courts. The report is limited to a discussion of Congress's participation in litigation as either a plaintiff (e.g., the party initiating the suit alleging some sort of harm or violation of law) or as a third-party intervener (e.g., a party who is seeking to join litigation already initiated by another plaintiff). The report does not address situations where Congress or individual Members appear as a defendant, or congressional participation in court cases as *amicus curiae* ("friend of the court"), as those situations do not raise the same legal and constitutional questions as does the involvement of Congress or its Members as a party plaintiff.

Generally, to participate as party litigants, congressional plaintiffs, whether they be individual Members, committees, Houses of Congress (i.e., the House or Senate), or legislative branch entities, must demonstrate that they meet the constitutional requirements established by Article III of the Constitution. Specifically, the prospective congressional plaintiff must show that he has standing to sue and that the court has the proper jurisdiction to adjudicate the claim. The failure to show either standing and/or jurisdiction is fatal to the litigation and will result in its dismissal without a decision by the court on the merits of the presented claims. With respect to the ability of Congress and Members to demonstrate Article III standing, the Supreme Court's 1997 decision in *Raines v. Byrd* has had a chilling effect on the ability of individual Members of Congress to adjudicate claims before federal courts. Despite the Court's holding in *Raines*, in 2008 the House Judiciary Committee, acting on a resolution from the full House of Representatives, was able to convince the US District Court for the District of Columbia that it had standing to sue the White House for its failure to make subpoenaed witnesses and documents available. In its decision, the court emphasized the distinction between suits brought by individual congressional plaintiffs asserting abstract and diffuse injuries and suits brought by organs of Congress alleging institutional harms.

Recent case law in this area suggests that suits brought by Congress in an institutional capacity have a far greater chance of being decided on their merits than do cases where individual Members attempt to assert personal or political injuries based on executive action. Through the years, Congress has had a fair amount of success intervening as a third party in ongoing litigation when it asserts a strong institutional interest in the case. This appears to be largely due to the fact that the jurisdiction of the court, and not Article III standing, has been the focal point of the court's analysis.

Chapter 2 - Savvy criminals constantly develop new techniques to target US persons, businesses, and interests. Central to the evolution of modern-day crime are four broad operational realities—geographic borders, criminal turf, cyberspace, and law enforcement jurisdiction. Individual criminals as well as broad criminal networks exploit these realities and often leverage the unique characteristics of one against the other to dodge law enforcement countermeasures and efforts to disrupt illicit activity. Further, the *interplay* of these realities can potentially encumber policing measures. In light of these interwoven realities, policy makers may question how to best design policies to help law enforcement combat ever-evolving criminal threats.

Chapter 3 - Many Indian tribes have tribal court systems where tribal laws and regulations may be enforced against tribal members. However, absent express congressional authorization, a tribal court may subject nonmembers to its civil jurisdiction for claims arising from non-Indian fee lands located within Indian reservations only if (1) the nonmember has entered into a consensual commercial relationship with the tribe or a tribal member, or (2) the conduct of the nonmember has some direct effect on the political integrity, economic security, or the health or welfare of the tribe. The Supreme Court addressed the reach of tribal civil jurisdiction over nonmembers in *Plains Commerce Bank v. Long Family Land and Cattle Co., Inc.*, 554 US ___, 128 S. Ct. 2709 (2008), a case that presents the question of whether Indian tribal courts have jurisdiction over a nonmember involved in a civil tort claim arising out of a consensual business relationship with a tribal member. In this case, tribal members had alleged that an off-reservation bank had discriminated against them by refusing to sell back land that the tribal members had previously owned and sold to the bank pursuant to a mortgage agreement. In tribal court, the tribal members brought an array of tribal common law claims, and won most of them, including the discrimination claim. The Supreme Court, however, reversed, holding that tribes cannot regulate or adjudicate claims relating to the sale of non-Indian fee lands.

Chapter 4 - The US military justice system exercises jurisdiction over criminal cases pursuant to Article I of the US Constitution and the Uniform Code of Military Justice (UCMJ). Military courts' jurisdiction is limited to trying people connected to the armed forces for crimes defined by the UCMJ. Within these constraints, military courts' jurisdiction is relatively broad. For example, it extends to retired servicemembers such as the defendant in *United States v. Stevenson*, a case in which military courts convicted a man on the Navy's temporary disability retired list. In *Stevenson*, the Navy prosecuted the defendant for rape, a crime routinely tried in non-military courts with civilian defendants.

Chapter 5 - Although an author need not register his or her work with the US Copyright Office to obtain copyright protection, registration is a statutory prerequisite to bringing suit for infringement of the copyright, as mandated by 17 USC. §411(a). The question in *Reed Elsevier, Inc. v. Muchnick* is whether this section of the Copyright Act restricts the subject-matter jurisdiction of the federal courts over copyright infringement claims involving unregistered works.

Chapter 6 - This report discusses recent legislation and decisions by the Government Accountability Office (GAO) and the US Court of Federal Claims regarding jurisdiction over orders issued under civilian agency contracts. On December 31, 2011, President Obama signed legislation that effectively overturned two recent decisions by GAO and the Court of Federal Claims finding that they have jurisdiction over protests challenging the issuance of task and delivery orders of any size under civilian agency contracts, even if these orders do not increase the scope, period, or maximum value of the underlying contract. Prior to these decisions, executive branch agencies and many commentators had construed the Federal Acquisition Streamlining Act (FASA) of 1994, as amended by the National Defense Authorization Act (NDAA) for FY2008, as authorizing only protests concerning the issuance of orders under civilian agency contracts that (1) increased the scope, period, or maximum value of the underlying contract or (2) were valued in excess of $10 million, as well as granting GAO temporary exclusive jurisdiction over protests involving the latter. However, GAO and the court rejected this interpretation, finding that what expired on May 27, 2011, were limitations on their jurisdiction imposed by FASA, as amended by the NDAA for FY2008. Thus, they concluded that they and, potentially, procuring agencies had jurisdiction over protests of orders of any size issued under the contracts of civilian agencies, regardless of whether these orders increased the scope, period, or maximum value of the underlying contract.

In: Jurisdiction ISBN: 978-1-62081-429-1
Editors: A. Stewart and D. Washington 

*Chapter 1*

# CONGRESSIONAL PARTICIPATION IN ARTICLE III COURTS: JURISDICTION AND STANDING TO SUE*

***Todd B. Tatelman***

## SUMMARY

As disputes between Congress and the executive become more prevalent, questions about Congress's ability to turn to the federal courts for vindication of its powers and prerogatives, or for declarations that the executive is in violation of the law or the Constitution, begin to arise. This report seeks to provide an overview of Congress's ability to participate in litigation before Article III courts. The report is limited to a discussion of Congress's participation in litigation as either a plaintiff (e.g., the party initiating the suit alleging some sort of harm or violation of law) or as a third-party intervener (e.g., a party who is seeking to join litigation already initiated by another plaintiff). The report does not address situations where Congress or individual Members appear as a defendant, or congressional participation in court cases as *amicus curiae* ("friend of the court"), as those situations do not raise the same legal and constitutional questions as does the involvement of Congress or its Members as a party plaintiff.

---

* This is an edited, reformatted and augmented version of the Congressional Research Service Publication, CRS Report for Congress R40873, dated October 26, 2009.

Generally, to participate as party litigants, congressional plaintiffs, whether they be individual Members, committees, Houses of Congress (i.e., the House or Senate), or legislative branch entities, must demonstrate that they meet the constitutional requirements established by Article III of the Constitution. Specifically, the prospective congressional plaintiff must show that he has standing to sue and that the court has the proper jurisdiction to adjudicate the claim. The failure to show either standing and/or jurisdiction is fatal to the litigation and will result in its dismissal without a decision by the court on the merits of the presented claims. With respect to the ability of Congress and Members to demonstrate Article III standing, the Supreme Court's 1997 decision in *Raines v. Byrd* has had a chilling effect on the ability of individual Members of Congress to adjudicate claims before federal courts.

Despite the Court's holding in *Raines*, in 2008 the House Judiciary Committee, acting on a resolution from the full House of Representatives, was able to convince the US District Court for the District of Columbia that it had standing to sue the White House for its failure to make subpoenaed witnesses and documents available. In its decision, the court emphasized the distinction between suits brought by individual congressional plaintiffs asserting abstract and diffuse injuries and suits brought by organs of Congress alleging institutional harms.

Recent case law in this area suggests that suits brought by Congress in an institutional capacity have a far greater chance of being decided on their merits than do cases where individual Members attempt to assert personal or political injuries based on executive action.

Through the years, Congress has had a fair amount of success intervening as a third party in ongoing litigation when it asserts a strong institutional interest in the case. This appears to be largely due to the fact that the jurisdiction of the court, and not Article III standing, has been the focal point of the court's analysis.

## INTRODUCTION

As disputes between Congress and the executive become more prevalent, questions about Congress's ability to turn to the federal courts for vindication of its powers and prerogatives, or for declarations that the executive is in violation of the law or the Constitution, begin to arise. This report seeks to provide an overview of Congress's ability to participate in litigation before Article III courts. The report is limited to a discussion of Congress's participation in litigation as either a plaintiff (e.g., the party initiating the suit alleging some sort of harm or violation of law) or as a third-party intervener (e.g., a party who is seeking to join litigation already initiated by another plaintiff). The report does not address situations where Congress or individual Members appear as a defendant, or congressional participation in court cases as *amicus curiae* ("friend of the court"), as those situations do not raise the same legal and constitutional questions as does the involvement of Congress or its Members as a party plaintiff.

Generally, to participate as party litigants, congressional plaintiffs, whether they be individual Members, committees, Houses of Congress (i.e., the House or Senate), or legislative branch entities, must demonstrate that they meet the constitutional requirements established by Article III of the Constitution. Specifically, the prospective congressional plaintiff must show that he has standing to sue and that the court has the proper jurisdiction to adjudicate the claim. The failure to show either standing and/or jurisdiction is fatal to the litigation and will result in its dismissal without a decision by the court on the merits of the presented claims. With respect to the ability of Congress and Members to demonstrate Article III standing, the Supreme Court's 1997 decision in *Raines v. Byrd* has had a chilling effect on the ability of individual Members of Congress to adjudicate claims before federal courts.

Despite the Court's holding in *Raines*, in 2008 the House Judiciary Committee, acting on a resolution from the full House of Representatives, was able to convince the US District Court for the District of Columbia that it had standing to sue the White House for its failure to make subpoenaed witnesses and documents available. In its decision, the court emphasized the distinction between suits brought by individual congressional plaintiffs asserting abstract and diffuse injuries and suits brought by organs of Congress alleging institutional harms.

Recent case law in this area suggests that suits brought by Congress in an institutional capacity have a far greater chance of being decided on their merits than do cases where individual Members attempt to assert personal or political injuries based on executive action. Through the years, Congress has had a fair amount of success intervening as a third party in ongoing litigation when it asserts a strong institutional interest in the case. This appears to be largely due to the fact that the jurisdiction of the court, and not Article III standing, has been the focal point of the court's analysis.

## Article III Standing

Generally, the doctrine of standing is a threshold procedural question that does not turn on the merits of a plaintiff's complaint, but rather on whether the particular plaintiff has a legal right to a judicial determination on the issues before the court.[1] The law with respect to standing is a mix of both constitutional requirements and prudential considerations.[2]

Article III of the Constitution specifically limits the exercise of federal judicial power to "cases" and "controversies";[3] thus, it has been said that "the law of Article III standing is built on a single basic idea—the idea of separation of powers."[4]

According to the Supreme Court, to satisfy the constitutional standing requirements of Article III, "[a] plaintiff must allege personal injury fairly traceable to the defendant's allegedly unlawful conduct and likely to be redressed by the requested relief."[5]

In addition to the constitutional questions posed by the doctrine of standing, federal courts have also adhered to a well-developed set of prudential principles that are relevant to a standing inquiry.[6] Similar to the constitutional requirements, these "judicially self-imposed limits on the exercise of federal jurisdiction," are "founded in concern about the proper—and properly limited—role of the courts in a democratic society."[7] However, unlike their constitutional counterparts, prudential standing requirements "can be modified or abrogated by Congress."[8]

The prudential components of the doctrine of standing require that (1) a plaintiff assert his own legal rights and interests rather than those of third parties; (2) a plaintiff's complaint be encompassed by the "zone of interests" protected or regulated by the constitutional or statutory guarantee at issue; and (3) courts decline to adjudicate "abstract questions of wide public significance which amount to generalized grievances pervasively shared and most appropriately addressed in the representative branches."[9]

## Participation of Individual Members of Congress before the Courts

As applied to congressional plaintiffs, the doctrine of standing has generally been invoked only in cases involving challenges to actions of the executive branch or to acts of Congress. Prior to the Supreme Court's 1997 decision in *Raines v. Byrd*,[10] the case law with respect to the standing of Members of Congress had been largely, though not exclusively, developed by decisions of the United States Court of Appeals for the D.C. Circuit.[11]

## Individual Member Standing Prior to *Raines v. Byrd*

Before *Raines v. Byrd* was decided in 1997, the D.C. Circuit relied on two Supreme Court decisions in developing the law of legislative standing. The first case, *Coleman v. Miller*,[12] involved the ratification of a constitutional amendment by the state legislature of Kansas. *Coleman* was initiated by 24 members of the Kansas legislature, who asserted that the lieutenant governor, by casting the tie-breaking vote regarding ratification of a proposed amendment to the US Constitution concerning child labor practices, had acted beyond the scope of his authority and, therefore, the court should order the secretary of state to erase the state's ratification of the amendment.[13] The Kansas supreme court rejected the request, holding that the lieutenant governor was authorized to cast the tie-breaking vote to ratify the amendment.[14] On appeal to the United States Supreme Court, the Kansas attorney general argued that the legislators lacked standing to challenge the ratification. The Court, addressing the standing argument, held that the legislators had a "plain, direct and adequate interest in maintaining the effectiveness of their votes[,]" and thus, had standing under Article III.[15] In addition, the Court reasoned that these legislators supported a claim under the Constitution to have their votes given full effect, and that the state court denied their rights.[16] Therefore, the Court declared that the legislators, if their contentions proved true, had a sufficient interest in the controversy.[17] Despite holding that the legislators had standing, the Court affirmed the holding of the Kansas supreme court. According to the Court, because Article V of the Constitution grants undivided power to Congress to control the amendment process, questions regarding ratification of constitutional amendments are "political questions" and, therefore, non-justiciable.[18]

The second major case relied upon by the D.C. Circuit was *Powell v. McCormack.*[19] *Powell* involved a challenge by Representative Adam Clayton Powell, Jr., that he was unconstitutionally excluded from the House of Representatives and, therefore, deprived of his federal salary. The Court held that Representative Powell had standing because he was able to demonstrate a private, personal injury not merely an institutionally related one. As the Supreme Court would later note in *Raines v. Byrd*, Powell's injury really involved the "loss of [a] private right"—his right to his seat and salary—and not the "loss of political power."[20]

Given the limited precedent from the Supreme Court, decisions from the D.C. Circuit have been the principal source of jurisprudence regarding the standing of individual Members of Congress to bring civil suits in federal court. Though not the only federal appeals court to hear such cases, the D.C. Circuit has since the 1970s developed several varying approaches to the issue. The first approach arose in *Mitchell v. Laird*,[21] which involved a suit by 12 Members of the House of Representatives against President Richard Nixon and the Secretaries of State, Defense, and the military branches, alleging that they were conducting an unconstitutional military operation in Southeast Asia because Congress had never expressly declared war.[22] In granting the Members standing, the D.C. Circuit adopted a broad theory, best described as the "bears upon" test.[23] The court concluded that because a judicial declaration that the defendants were operating beyond the scope of their constitutional duties "would bear upon the duties of the [Members] to consider whether to impeach defendants and upon [the Members] quite distinct and different duties to make appropriations to support the hostilities, or to take other actions to support the hostilities …," the Members had sufficient interest to have standing.[24] Although the court would ultimately dismiss the case on political question grounds without deciding the merits, the rationale for legislator standing remained as the law of the circuit and arguably provided fodder for additional lawsuits by Members against other government officials.[25]

Beginning in 1974, the D.C. Circuit issued a series of opinions that rejected the "bears upon" test and changed the standard for legislator standing. The first of these cases, *Kennedy v. Sampson*,[26] involved a suit by Senator Edward M. Kennedy against the General Services Administration requiring it to take the necessary steps to certify that the Family Practice Medicine Act had become federal law. Although the bill had passed both houses of Congress and had been presented to the President, Congress had recessed prior to the elapsing of the 10 days that the President had to sign or veto the bill. President Nixon refused to sign the bill into law and argued that because Congress was not in session, the bill failed to become law by virtue of a "pocket veto."[27] Senator Kennedy asserted that the language in the Constitution authorizing a "pocket veto" only applied to end-of-session adjournments, and not intra-session recesses of the Congress.[28]

Prior to reaching the merits,[29] the court addressed Senator Kennedy's Article III standing. The court put forth two approaches to adjudicating such claims, neither of which was the "bears upon" test. The first, according to the court, was to inquire "whether a 'logical nexus' exists between the status asserted by a litigant and the claim sought to be adjudicated."[30] The court found that such a "logical nexus" existed, concluding that Members of Congress can challenge "the validity of executive action which purports to have disapproved of an Act of Congress by means of a constitutional procedure which does not permit Congress to override the disapproval."[31] The court's second approach required questioning whether the plaintiff, in this case Senator Kennedy, alleged that the action caused him "'injury in fact,' economic or otherwise" and whether "the interest sought to be protected [is] 'arguably within the zone of interests to be protected or regulated by the statute or constitutional guarantee in question.'"[32] The court concluded that the injury to Senator Kennedy denied him the effectiveness of his vote as a United States Senator and that it was within the "zone of interest" protected by Article I, Section 7 of the Constitution.[33] Finally, the court addressed a question left from the Supreme Court's decision in *Coleman v. Miller*; namely, can only one or several legislators have standing, or must the entire legislature, in this case Congress, be before the court? The Nixon Administration had argued that "only the interests of the Congress or one of its Houses as a body are protected by this provision." The court rejected the Administration's reading of *Coleman*, holding that "the better reasoned view of both *Coleman* and the present case is that an individual legislator has standing to protect the effectiveness of his vote with or without the concurrence of other members of the majority."[34]

Subsequently, in both *Harrington v. Bush*,[35] and *Goldwater v. Carter*,[36] the D.C. Circuit further refined its approach to legislative standing cases. *Harrington* involved a suit by Congressman Michael Harrington seeking a declaratory judgment that the Central Intelligence Agency was engaging in illegal activities. The court, in deciding that Congressman Harrington did not have standing, clearly stated that "[t]he most basic point to consider is that there are no special standards for determining Congressional standing questions."[37] According to the court, although congressional plaintiffs may have issues and concerns that are unique, the legal approach for examining those issues is the same and it requires that a party allege "a distinct and palpable injury to himself."[38] In determining whether Congressman Harrington met this standard, the court adopted the approach from *Kennedy*, which "relies on nullification of a specific vote as the requisite injury in fact."[39] Using this standard, the court found that Harrington was not injured because neither future votes on matters related to funding the CIA were impaired, nor was his effectiveness as a legislator objectively diminished.[40]

The D.C. Circuit continued this line of reasoning in *Goldwater v. Carter*.[41] This time focusing on what was meant by disenfranchisement of a Member's right to vote. Senator Goldwater brought suit against President Carter over the unilateral termination of the Mutual Defense Treaty with the Republic of China (Taiwan). According to Senator Goldwater, the President's action was unconstitutional because he did not submit the treaty to the Senate for a vote on its termination. Thus, the Senator suffered an "injury in fact" because he was completely denied the right to vote on the treaty's termination. The court agreed, noting that "to be cognizable for standing purposes the alleged diminution in congressional influence must amount to a disenfranchisement, a complete nullification or withdrawal of a voting opportunity; and the plaintiff must point to an objective standard in the Constitution, statutes, or congressional house rules, by which disenfranchisement can be shown."[42] In concluding that Senator Goldwater had been so disenfranchised, the court set forth the standard for determining when such nullification occurs. According to the court, "[w]hether the President's action amounts to a complete disenfranchisement depends on whether [the Members] have left to them any legislative means to vote in the way they claim is their right."[43]

After the court's decision in *Goldwater*, it appeared that the law of legislator standing was settled. Legislators seeking to bring suit in federal court had to demonstrate a concrete injury in fact resulting in the complete disenfranchisement of their right to vote. In addition, a Member must show that no other legislative remedies are available. The mere fact that the executive had violated the law arguably was no longer sufficient, nor was mere diminishment in effectiveness as a Member of Congress. Further, the court established that it did not matter whether one or several legislators brought the suit, as it was not required that either the entire Congress or even a single House be a party.

The settled nature of the law, however, did not last long. In 1979, Senator Donald Riegle brought suit against the Federal Open Market Committee, arguing that it was unconstitutionally constituted because its appointees were not submitted to the Senate for its "advice and consent." In *Riegle v. Federal Open Market Committee*,[44] the D.C. Circuit concluded that, if a Member of Congress can establish standing under the rules applied in non-congressional plaintiff cases, the separation of powers issues raised by the Member's suit are most properly addressed by an application of what it called the "doctrine of circumscribed equitable discretion."[45] As explained by the court, this prudential doctrine requires that suits brought by Members of Congress be dismissed only if the Member has a legislative remedy and a similar action could be brought by a private plaintiff.[46] The "legislative remedy" aspect of this doctrine seems to reflect a judicial reluctance to provide a forum to a Member who has failed to exhaust possible legislative avenues of relief, or who has done so unsuccessfully.[47]

After *Riegle*, it appears that Members had some success in establishing standing, but such suits were frequently dismissed on the basis of the equitable discretion doctrine.[48] The problems presented by congressional plaintiff suits were explained by the D.C. Circuit in an important post-*Riegle* ruling, *Moore v. US House of Representatives*:

> Suits against coordinate branches of government by congressional plaintiffs pose separation-of-powers concerns which may affect a complainant's standing to invoke the jurisdiction of the federal courts. To the extent that the Constitution envisions limited federal court jurisdiction out of respect for the coordinate branches of government, we have been reluctant to grant standing to members of Congress alleging generalized, amorphous injuries due to either the actions of their colleagues in Congress or the conduct of the Executive.... [W]here separation-of-powers concernsare present,the plaintiff's alleged injury must bespecificand cognizable in order to give rise to standing.... Deprivation of a constitutionally mandated process of enacting law may inflict a more specific injury on a member of Congress than would be presented by a generalized complaint that a legislator's effectiveness is diminished by allegedly illegal activities taking place outside the legislative forum.[49]

## Raines v. Byrd

In 1997, the Supreme Court decided *Raines v. Byrd*,[50] which presented a constitutional challenge to the Line Item Veto Act of 1996.[51] The Court, in an opinion by Chief Justice Rehnquist, held that plaintiffs, all of whom were Members of Congress who had voted against the act, lacked standing because their complaint did not establish that they had suffered an injury that was personal, particularized, and concrete.[52] Although the holding was based on the Court's finding that plaintiffs did not satisfy the personal injury requirement of standing, the Court also questioned whether the plaintiffs could meet the second standing requirement; namely, that the injury be "fairly traceable" to unlawful conduct by the defendants "since the alleged cause of ... [plaintiffs'] injury is not ... [the executive branch defendants'] exercise of legislative power but the actions of their own colleagues in Congress in passing the act."[53] The majority opinion distinguished between a personal injury to a private right, such as the loss of salary presented in *Powell v.*

*McCormack*,[54] and an institutional or official injury.[55] The Court held that a congressional plaintiff may have standing in a suit against the executive branch if it is alleged that the plaintiff(s) have suffered either a personal injury (e.g., loss of a Member's seat) or an institutional one[56] that is not "abstract and widely dispersed," but rather amounts to vote nullification.[57] In *Raines*, the Court concluded that the plaintiffs' votes were not nullified due to the continued existence of other legislative remedies. As the Court explained,

> They have not alleged that they voted for a specific bill, that there were sufficient votes to pass the bill, and that the bill was nonetheless deemed defeated. In the vote on the Line Item Veto Act, their votes were given full effect. They simply lost that vote. Nor can they allege that the Act will nullify their votes in the future in the same way that the votes of the *Coleman* legislators had been nullified. In the future, a majority of Senators and Congressman can pass or reject appropriations bills.... In addition, a majority ofSenatorsand Congressman can vote to repeal the Act, or to exempt a given appropriations bill (or a given provision in an appropriations bill) from the Act.... Coleman thus provides little meaningful precedent for appellees' argument.[58]

As a result, under *Raines* it appears that a congressional plaintiff is more likely to succeed in establishing standing where there is an allegation of a particular personal injury, as opposed to an injury related to either a generalized grievance about the conduct of government, or an injury amounting to a claim of diminished effectiveness as a legislator.[59] While the Court in *Raines* seemed prepared to recognize the standing of a Member based on a personal injury to a private right, it nevertheless concluded that an injury to a legislator's voting power is an institutional or official injury.[60]

Furthermore, it appears that the limits on Member standing established in *Raines* will likely preclude a Member from obtaining standing in a suit to challenge an act of Congress[61] because of the availability of legislative remedies, including, but not limited to, the repeal or amendment of the act in question,[62] which would prevent a court from finding vote nullification. In addition, though the Court did not expressly overrule *Coleman, Kennedy,* or *Riegle*, *Raines* appears to restrict "standing to challenge executive action, although there may be a better opportunity to achieve standing in this setting."[63] This is arguably the case in situations where a plaintiff Member can show the nullification of a vote by the executive and, thus, establish an institutional injury.[64]

# CONGRESSIONAL STANDING AFTER *RAINES V. BYRD*

## Suits by Individual Members

Decisions of the D.C. Circuit involving individual Members of Congress that have followed *Raines* have attempted to clarify both the meaning of "nullification," as well as the status of pre-*Raines* rulings by the D.C. Circuit. With respect to the status of its pre-*Raines* rulings, a majority of the D.C. Circuit in *Chenoweth v. Clinton* concluded that the Supreme Court's decision in *Raines* limited but has not overruled its precedents.[65] *Chenoweth* involved a dispute between then President Clinton and several members of Congress over the implementation of a historic preservation program that was established via executive order and without statutory authorization. The Members brought suit, arguing that

> the President's issuance of the [ ] executive order, without statutory authority therefore, deprived [the plaintiffs] of their constitutionally guaranteedresponsibilityof open debateand vote on issues and legislation involving interstate commerce, federal lands, the expenditure of federal monies, and implementation of [the National Environmental Protection Act].[66]

Relying on *Raines*, the court denied the Members standing, holding that the alleged injury did not rise to the level of vote nullification required by the Court's decision.[67] The case, however, presented a conflict between the Court's holding in *Raines* and the precedents of the D.C. Circuit established by *Kennedy, Goldwater, Moore,* and subsequent cases. Rather than expressly overruling its previous cases, the D.C. Circuit hedged, pulling back on its expansive standing determination in *Kennedy* and *Moore* and suggesting that the portion of the court's jurisprudence regarding the availability of legislative remedies merely be reincorporated into its more general standing analysis like it had been in *Goldwater.*[68]

In 2000, the D.C. Circuit decided *Campbell v. Clinton* [69] and more directly addressed the meaning of the term "vote nullification." *Campbell* was a suit filed by 31 Members of Congress seeking a declaration that President Clinton violated the War Powers Clause of the Constitution and the War Powers Resolution by directing United States forces' participation in North Atlantic Treaty Organization (NATO) airstrikes against the Federal Republic of Yugoslavia without congressional authorization.[70] In support of their position, the Members attempted to fit the case into the *Coleman* exception to *Raines* by arguing that their votes defeating a War Powers Resolution and congressional declaration of war were "nullified" by the continued involvement of US troops.[71] The court rejected this argument and interpreted the *Raines* notion of vote nullification to mean that no other legislative remedies are available to rectify the action by the executive. According to the court, what distinguishes the situation in *Coleman* from that in *Raines* is that

> [t]he *Coleman* senators, … may well have been powerless to rescind a ratification of a constitutional amendment that they claimed had been defeated. In other words, they had no legislative remedy. Under that reading—which we think explains the very narrow possible *Coleman* exception to *Raines*—appellants fail because they continued, after the votes, to enjoy ample legislative power to have stopped prosecution of the "war."
>
> In this case, Congress certainly could have passed a law forbidding the use of US forces in the Yugoslav campaign; indeed, there was a measure—albeit only a concurrent resolution— introduced to require the President to withdraw US troops.[72]

Thus, like the Senators in *Raines*, who could have repealed the Line Item Veto Act or exempted future appropriations bills from its application, the Members in *Campbell* had additional remedies available to them via the legislative process, therefore no vote nullification had occurred and no standing before a court generated.

## Institutional Suits

The first post-*Raines* attempt by the legislative branch to utilize the courts to resolve an institutional dispute with the executive branch occurred in 2002 when the then-General Accounting Office (GAO) filed a suit in federal district court for the District of Columbia, pursuant to its authority under 31 USC. § 716(b)(2), seeking to obtain records regarding the National Energy Policy Development Group (NEPDG).[73] GAO had been asked in 2001 by

Representative Henry Waxman and Representative John Dingell, then members of the minority party, that it initiate an investigation regarding the NEPDG's activities, based upon reports that task force meetings included "exclusive groups of non-governmental participants."[74] Subsequent to initiating its investigation, GAO requested information from the Vice President regarding the names and titles of individuals present at any NEPDG meetings, including any non-governmental participants, as well as information pertaining to the purpose and agenda of the meetings, the process by which the NEPDG determined who would be invited to such meetings, and whether minutes or notes were kept.[75] After several attempts to obtain the requested information were unsuccessful, GAO issued a demand letter pursuant to 31 USC. §716(b), requesting the aforementioned records, including copies of the minutes and notes of the meetings, as well as any information presented by private sector attendees.[76]

The court in *Walker* dismissed GAO's suit after determining that the Comptroller General lacked standing to sue under the principles and standards delineated in *Raines v. Byrd.*[77] Applying *Raines*, the court in *Walker* determined that it was required to conduct an "especially rigorous" standing inquiry because the case presented "core separation of powers questions at the heart of the relationship among the three branches of our government."[78] Engaging in this calculus, the court held that the injury alleged by the Comptroller General was not personal, stressing that his interest in the suit was "solely institutional, relating exclusively to his duties in his official capacity."[79] The court then determined that the institutional injury alleged by the Comptroller General, namely the Vice President's denial of information requested pursuant to GAO's statutorily conferred investigative and access enforcement authority, was insufficient to establish standing. The court predicated this finding on its conclusion that the Comptroller General was acting as an agent of Congress in demanding the information and bringing the suit, and had no "freestanding institutional injury or personal injury of his own to assert."[80] The court then reiterated that the jurisdiction of the federal courts "can be invoked only when the plaintiff himself has suffered some threatened or actual injury."[81]

In reaching this conclusion, the court in *Walker* found it to be of "some importance" that Congress had not expressly authorized the present suit, and determined that a generalized delegation of investigative and access enforcement authority to GAO was not sufficiently specific to provide a basis for the Comptroller General to seek judicial resolution of the significant constitutional issues raised by the suit.[82] In particular, while stressing that it did not "intend to direct the delegation and exercise of Congress's investigative powers,"[83] the court held that the "highly generalized allocation of enforcement power to the Comptroller General ... hardly gives this Court confidence that the current Congress has authorized this Comptroller General to pursue a judicial resolution of the specific issues affecting the balance of power between the Article I and Article II Branches that have crystallized during the course of this dispute and lawsuit."[84] Based on these factors, the court concluded that the exercise of judicial power in this case was not "warranted as a 'last resort, and as a necessity,'" and declined to address the merits of the suit.[85]

Finally, the 2008 opinion by the US District Court for the District of Columbia in *Committee on Judiciary, US House of Representatives v. Miers*, [86] arguably limits the effect of *Raines* and *Walker* on other situations involving institutional litigation efforts by the Congress. *Miers* involved a civil suit brought by the House Judiciary Committee seeking to enforce subpoenas against specific former and current White House officials. The district court held that unlike the GAO in *Walker*, the Judiciary Committee "had been expressly authorized by the House of Representatives *as an institution*" to bring the suit.[87] That simple factual distinction, according to the court, "moves this case from the impermissible category of an individual plaintiff asserting an institutional injury (*Raines, Walker*) to the permissible category of an institutional plaintiff asserting an institutional injury (*AT&T I, Senate Select Committee*)"[88] and, therefore, preserves the committee's standing under Article III.

## THE JURISDICTION OF ARTICLE III COURTS

In addition to satisfying the standing requirements of Article III, potential congressional plaintiffs must demonstrate that the federal courts have the proper jurisdiction to decide the dispute. The jurisdiction of federal courts, specifically federal district courts, where a civil action by Congress, a single House of Congress, congressional committee, individual Member, or legislative branch entity would likely be brought, is derived from both Article III of the Constitution and federal statute. Article III of the Constitution states, in relevant part, that "[t]he Judicial Power shall extend to all Cases, in Law and Equity, arising under this Constitution, the Laws of the United States."[89] The Supreme Court has interpreted the language "arising under" broadly, essentially permitting federal jurisdiction to be found whenever federal law "is a potentially important ingredient of a case."[90] Conversely, the federal question jurisdiction statute, first enacted in 1875,[91] while containing almost identical language to Article III, has been interpreted by the Court to be much narrower in scope. As the Court explained in *Verlinden B.V. v. Central Bank of Nigeria*,

> Although the language of 1331 parallels that of the "Arising Under" Clause of Art. III, thisCourt never has held that statutory "arising under" jurisdiction is identical to Art. III "arising under" jurisdiction. Quite the contrary is true.... [T]he many limitations which have been placed on jurisdiction under 1331 arenot limitations on the constitutional powerofCongress to confer jurisdiction on the federal courts.... Art. III "arising under" jurisdiction is broader than federal-question jurisdiction under 1331.[92]

The fact that the statutory jurisdiction currently provided by Congress is narrower than the Constitution's grant of judicial power may give rise to an argument suggesting that the existing statutory grant of jurisdiction cannot be used as the basis for a lawsuit filed by a congressional plaintiff. Following this argument to its conclusion suggests that before any civil action by a congressional plaintiff can be initiated, both Houses of Congress must pass, and the President must sign into law, a statute authorizing such an action to be brought in federal district court. Pursuant to this line of reasoning, other forms of authorization, such as a one-House resolution, would not be sufficient to provide federal court jurisdiction.

## PARTICIPATION OF THE CONGRESS AS AN INSTITUTION

Although there does not appear to be any court or commentator that has expressly adopted the jurisdictional argument made above, it remains unclear whether the existing statutory language for jurisdiction can be definitively said to be adequate. Rather, the limited Supreme Court and other federal court precedent that exists may be read to suggest that the current statutory basis is sufficient to establish jurisdiction for a civil action if the congressional plaintiff is specifically authorized by a house of Congress to act.

In 1928, the Supreme Court decided *Reed v. The County Commissioners of Delaware County, Pennsylvania,*[93] which involved a special committee of the United States Senate charged, by Senate resolution, with investigating the means used to influence the nomination of candidates for the Senate.[94] The special committee was authorized to "require by subpoena or otherwise the attendance of witnesses, the production of books, papers, and documents, and to do such other acts as may be necessary in the matter of said investigation."[95] During the course of its investigation into the disputed election of William B. Wilson of Pennsylvania to the Senate, the committee sought to obtain the "boxes, ballots, and other things used in connection with the election."[96] The County Commissioners of Delaware County, who were the legal custodians of said materials, refused to provide them to the committee, thus necessitating litigation. The Supreme Court, after affirming the powers of the Senate to "obtain evidence related to matter committed to it by the Constitution"[97] and having "passed laws calculated to facilitate such investigations,"[98] nevertheless held that it was without jurisdiction to decide the case. The Senate had relied on the resolution's phrase "such other acts as may be necessary" to justify their authority to bring such a suit. According to the Court, however, that phrase "may not be taken to include everything that under any circumstances might be covered by its words."[99] As a result, the Court held that "the Senate did not intend to authorize the committee, or anticipate that there might be need, to invoke the power of the Judicial Department. Petitioners are not 'authorized by law to sue.'"[100] The Court in *Reed* made no mention of the jurisdictional statute that existed at the time. Rather, the Court appears to have relied on the fact that the Senate did not specifically authorize the committee to sue; therefore, absent particular language granting the power to sue in court, there can be no basis for judicial jurisdiction over such a suit. Read in this manner, *Reed* appears to suggest that had the Senate resolution specifically mentioned the power to sue, the Court may have accepted jurisdiction and decided the case on its merits. Such a reading of *Reed* is supported by a recent district court ruling involving the question of whether Congress authorized judicial enforcement of Member demands for information from executive branch agencies.[101]

*Reed* stands for the proposition that Congress must expressly authorize the commencement of litigation to satisfy the court's jurisdictional concerns. The Court, however, was not specific with respect to how this authorization need be provided. Thus, the question arises as to whether a law—passed by both houses and signed by the President or his veto overridden—is required, or can the Congress use other methods, such as a concurrent resolution (H. Con. Res.) or even a one-house resolution? The argument that a one-house resolution is not sufficient to provide federal court jurisdiction derives support from the ruling in *Senate Select Committee on Presidential Campaign Activities v.*

*Nixon*,[102] a 1973 decision by the US District Court for the District of Columbia. The Select Committee was an organ of the Senate and exercised its power pursuant to a Senate resolution.[103] In *Senate Select Committee*, the court held that there was no jurisdictional statute available that authorizes the court to hear and decide the merits of the committee's request for a declaratory judgment, mandatory injunction, and writ of mandamus arising from President Nixon's refusal to produce tape recording and other documents sought by the committee pursuant to a *subpoena duces tecum*.[104] In reaching its conclusion, the court addressed several potential bases for jurisdiction: 28 USC. § 1345, United States as a Plaintiff; 28 USC. § 1361, Action to Compel an Officer of the United States to Perform His Duty; 5 USC. §§ 701-706, the Administrative Procedure Act; and, of particular relevance here, 28 USC. § 1331, the federal question jurisdiction statute.[105]

Focusing on 28 USC. § 1331, the court noted that the statute at the time contained a minimum "amount in controversy" requirement of "$10,000 exclusive of interest and costs."[106] The court stated that "[t]he satisfaction of a minimum amount-in-controversy is not a technicality; *it is a requirement imposed by Congress which the courts may not dispense with at their pleasure*."[107] Because the Select Committee could not establish a theory under which the amount in controversy requirement was satisfied, the court dismissed the case for lack of subject matter jurisdiction.[108]

Although *Senate Select Committee* may still be cited for the proposition that, absent a specific congressional enactment, Congress may not seek civil remedies in federal court, it is important to note that not only have subsequent cases held that "[w]here fundamental constitutional rights are involved, this court has been willing to find satisfaction of the jurisdictional amount requirement for federal question jurisdiction,"[109] but also that Congress specifically removed the amount in controversy requirement for federal question jurisdiction in 1980.[110] Given these developments, combined with the reading of *Reed v. County Commissioners* suggested above, it appears possible to argue that a specifically authorized congressional committee may bring a civil action to enforce a subpoena using 28 USC. § 1331 as a basis for federal question jurisdiction. In fact, such an argument has been suggested by a California district court in the 2006 case *Waxman v. Thompson*, which involved litigation initiated against the Secretary of the Department of Health and Human Services by several minority members of the House of Representatives pursuant to 5 USC. §§ 2954 and 7211—commonly referred to as the "rule of seven" statute.[111] According to the court in *Waxman*, the holdings of *Reed*, *Senate Select Committee* and *United States v. AT&T*[112]—

a case involving the intervention by a House committee chairman into a lawsuit by the Department of Justice who was attempting to enjoin compliance with a committee subpoena by AT&T—suggest that "legislative branch suits to enforce requests for information from the executive branch are justiciable *if authorized by one or both Houses of Congress*."[113]

Moreover, on several occasions the House of Representatives has authorized, via House resolution, the intervention by counsel representing a House committee into civil litigation. For example, in June of 1976, congressional subpoenas were issued to the American Telephone and Telegraph Company (AT&T) by the Subcommittee on Oversight and Investigations of the House Committee on Interstate and Foreign Commerce. The subcommittee was seeking copies of "all national security request letters sent to AT&T and its subsidiaries by the FBI as well as records of such taps prior to the time when the practice of sending such letters was initiated."[114] Before AT&T could comply with the request, the Department of Justice (DOJ) and the subcommittee's chairman, Representative John Moss, entered into negotiations seeking to reach an alternate agreement which would prevent AT&T from having to turn over all its records.[115] When these negotiations broke down, the DOJ sought an injunction in the US District Court for the District of Columbia prohibiting AT&T from complying with the subcommittee's subpoenas.

The House of Representatives responded to the litigation by authorizing Representative Moss to intervene in the suit on behalf of the Committee on Interstate and Foreign Commerce and the House of Representatives.[116] Specifically, the authorization for intervention was accomplished by House resolution, which provided that Chairman Moss was to represent the committee and the full House "to secure information relating to the privacy of telephone communications now in the possession of [AT&T] for the use of the Committee and the full House."[117] In addition, the resolution authorized Chairman Moss to hire a special counsel, use not more than $50,000 from the contingent fund of the committee to cover expenses, and to report to the full House on matters related as soon as practicable.[118] The resolution was adopted by the House by a vote of 180-108 on August 26, 1976.[119]

Chairman Moss's intervention into the proceedings was noted by the district court, and does not appear to have been contested by either AT&T or the DOJ.[120] Chairman Moss remained an intervener pursuant to the House resolution through the district court proceeding and two appeals to the US Court of Appeals for the District of Columbia Circuit until an agreement was reached with respect to the disclosure of the documents sought.

A second intervention authorization, this time involving litigation between Ashland Oil and the Federal Trade Commission (FTC), occurred in 1976. This case arose when Ashland Oil sought to enjoin the FTC from transferring its information to the Subcommittee on Oversight and Investigations of the Committee on Interstate and Foreign Commerce at the request of subcommittee Chairman Moss. When Ashland Oil obtained a temporary restraining order, the subcommittee promptly authorized a subpoena for the documents and Chairman Moss filed a resolution for authorization from the House to allow him to intervene with special counsel in the suit that Ashland Oil had filed seeking to enjoin the FTC from transferring the documents to the subcommittee.[121] The district court granted Chairman Moss's motion to intervene and ultimately refused to grant the injunction.[122] The court of appeals affirmed on the grounds that "no substantial showing was made that the materials in the possession of the FTC will necessarily be 'made public' if turned over to Congress."[123]

While *AT&T* and *Ashland Oil* represent affirmative authorizations for intervention by a House of Congress, *In Re Beef Industry Antitrust Litigation*[124] provides an example of what may occur should a house of Congress not provide express authorization to be represented in court. In *In Re Beef*, the chairmen of two subcommittees of the House of Representatives[125] sought to intervene in a pending antitrust dispute for the purpose of obtaining access to documents subpoenaed by subcommittees from a party to the litigation. The subpoenaed documents had been obtained through litigation discovery and were thus subject to a standing court protective order. The district court refused to modify its protective order allowing the party to comply with the subpoena.[126] The subcommittee chairmen appealed to the United States Court of Appeals for the Fifth Circuit.

On appeal, the Fifth Circuit entertained a motion to dismiss by one of the plaintiffs on the grounds that the chairmen had never obtained authorization from the full House of Representatives before filing their initial motion before the district court. The plaintiffs relied on what was then Rule XI, cl. 2(m)(2)(B) of the Rules of the House of Representatives, which provided that "[c]ompliance with any subpoena [sic] issued by a committee or subcommittee ... may be enforced only as authorized or directed by the House."[127] The subcommittee chairmen responded by arguing that the rule was not applicable as they were not seeking to enforce their subpoenas, but rather were seeking a modification of the district court's protective order.[128] Therefore, according to the chairmen, they did not require authorization from the full House of Representatives to appear in court.[129]

The Fifth Circuit rejected the chairmen's arguments, noting specifically that the House Rules "require[] House authorization not only for direct enforcement of a subpoena but also in any instance when a House committee seeks to institute or to intervene in litigation and, of course, to appeal from a court decision, particularly when the purpose is, as here, to obtain the effectuation of a subpoena."[130] The court also extensively relied on the *Ashland Oil* precedent, noting that similar to this case, the chairman in *Ashland Oil* was not seeking to enforce a subpoena, rather merely attempting to prevent an injunction from being issued.[131] The failure of the subcommittee chairmen to obtain an authorization resolution from the full House in this case necessitated the dismissal of their appeal without any decision on the merits.[132]

Finally, in *Waxman v. Thompson*, a 2006 opinion of the US District Court for the Central District of California,[133] the plaintiffs, all minority members of the House Government Reform Committee, sought a court order pursuant to 5 USC. §§ 2954 and 7211—often times referred to as the "rule of seven"—granting them access to Department of Health and Human Services records related to the anticipated costs of the Medicare Prescription Drug Improvement and Modernization Act of 2003.[134] The court, in dismissing the case for lack of jurisdiction, addressed the argument made by the plaintiffs that 5 USC. § 2954, which requires that "[a]n Executive agency, on request of the Committee on Government Operations of the House of Representatives, *or of any seven members thereof* ... shall submit any information requested of it relating to any matter within the jurisdiction of the committee,"[135] implicitly delegated to Members the right to sue to enforce their informational demands.[136] The court, in rejecting this argument, relied on the Supreme Court's holding in *Reed v. County Commissioners*.[137] Specifically, the court noted that *Reed*'s holding "put Congress on notice that it was necessary to make authorization to sue to enforce investigatory demands explicit if it wished to ensure that such power existed."[138] According to the court, like the Senate resolution at issue in *Reed*, because § 2954 is silent with respect to civil enforcement, it stands to reason that Congress never intended to provide the Members with the power to seek civil judicial orders to enforce their document demands.

From a jurisdictional standpoint, what appears to be required by the few cases on point is that the action by congressional representatives be expressly authorized. Whether this authorization comes in the form of a statute, joint resolution, concurrent resolution, or even a one-house resolution, appears not to be significant provided that it is express and unambiguous in its authorization for participation in federal court.

## CONCLUSION

Congress's ability to bring litigation before Article III courts remains severely limited by the Supreme Court's decision in *Raines v. Byrd.* For congressional suits to be successful, they must demonstrate either institutional injuries, such as refusal to comply with a duly authorized subpoena, or show complete vote nullification, meaning that no other legislative remedy can exist against the executive action they are challenging. Abstract and diffuse injuries such as diminution of status as a Member, or even deprivation of information needed to effectively legislate, are unlikely to result in Article III standing to sue. Consequently, it appears that the more successful suits will be brought by either Congress as a whole, a house of Congress, committees, and/or legislative branch institutions only when acting with the authorization of one or both houses of Congress. Because suits by individual Members require a much more stringent showing and, considering how rare it is for all legislative remedies to be foreclosed, therefore, after *Raines* and *Campbell*, it is unlikely that they will be successful.

## End Notes

[1] *See Flast v. Cohen*, 392 US 83, 99 (1968).

[2] *See Department of Commerce v. House of Representatives*, 525 US 316, 328-29 (1999). By law, Congress can granta right to sue to a plaintiff who would otherwise lack standing. According to the Court, however, such a law caneliminate only prudential, but not constitutional, standing requirements. *See Raines v. Byrd*, 521 US 811, 820 n.3(1997). For example, in the Line Item Veto Act, which was the statute at issue in *Raines*, Congress had grantedstanding to sue to "any Member of Congress or any individual adversely affected by" the act. *See* Line Item Veto Actof 1996, P.L. 104-130, § 692(a)(1), 110 Stat. 1200 (1996). Likewise, Congress also statutorily granted standing tochallenge the use of statistical sampling methods in the census. *See Department of Commerce v. House ofRepresentatives*, 525 US at 328-29.

[3] US CONST. Art. III, § 2 (stating that "The judicial Power shall extend to all *Cases*, in Law and Equity, arising underthis Constitution, the Laws of the United States, and Treaties made … under their Authority ... – to *Controversies* towhich the United States shall be a Party;– to *Controversies* between two or more States; ... .")(emphasis added).

[4] *Raines*, 521 US at 820 (*quoting Allen v. Wright*, 468 US 737, 752 (1984)).

[5] Department of Commerce v. United States House of Representatives, 525 US at 329 (internal quotations omitted).

[6] *Bennett v. Spear*, 520 US 154, 162 (1997).

[7] *Id.*

[8] *Id.*

[9] Valley Forge Christian College v. Americans United for the Separation of Church and State, 454 US 464, 474 (1982) (internal quotations omitted).

[10] 521 US 811 (1997).

[11] For cases heard outside the D.C. Circuit, *see, e.g., Holtzman v. Schlesinger*, 484 F.2d 1307 (2d Cir. 1973); *Ameron, Inc. v. United States Army Corps of Engineers*, 787 F.2d 875 (3d Cir. 1986); *Harrington v. Schlesinger*, 528 F.2d 455 (4th Cir. 1975); *Drummond v. Bunker*, 560 F.2d 625 (5th Cir. 1977); *Dole v. Carter*, 569 F.2d 1109 (10th Cir. 1977). In addition, there have been several cases that did not rise to the circuit court level. *See, e.g., Gravel v. Laird*, 347 F. Supp 7 (D.D.C. 1972); *Drinan v. Nixon*, 364 F. Supp 854 (D. Mass 1973); *Shaffer v. Clinton*, 54 F. Supp. 2d 1014 (D. Col. 1999). Finally, there was one case decided by a three-judge court, *McClure v. Carter*, 513 F. Supp. 265 (D. Idaho 1981), that was appealed directly to the Supreme Court, who affirmed the decision of the lower court to dismiss with no opinion. *See McClure v. Reagan*, 454 US 1025 (1981)(mem.).

[12] 307 US 433 (1939).

[13] *See id.* at 436.

[14] *See id.* at 437.

[15] *Id.* at 437-38.

[16] *Id.* at 438.

[17] *Id.* at 446.

[18] *See id.* at 450.

[19] 395 US 486 (1969).

[20] *Raines v. Byrd*, 521 US 811, 820-21 (1997).

[21] 488 F.2d 611 (D.C. Cir. 1973).

[22] *Id.* at 613.

[23] *See* Anthony Clark Arend & Catherine B. Lotrionte, *Congress Goes to Court: The Past, Present, and Future of Legislator Standing*, 25 HARV.J.L.& PUB.POL'Y 209, 223 (2002).

[24] *Id.* at 614.

[25] It should be noted that after *Mitchell*, both the Second and Fourth Circuits declined to follow the "bears upon" test in similar cases involving legislator standing. *See Holtzman v. Schlesinger*, 484 F.2d 207 (2d Cir. 1973) (suit brought by Representative Holtzman against the Secretary of Defense seeking an injunction against the use of force in Cambodia); *Harrington v. Schlesinger*, 528 F.2d 455 (4th Cir. 1975) (suit brought by Members of Congress, taxpayers, and citizens challenging expenditure of monies in support of military operations in Southeast Asia).

[26] 511 F.2d 430 (D.C. Cir. 1974).

[27] *Id.* at 436.

[28] *Id.* at 433.

[29] On the merits, the court concluded that the congressional recess did not prevent the President from returning the bill to Congress after his veto. As the constitutionally required 10-day period had elapsed without Presidential action, the bill was not considered to have been vetoed, but rather became law consistent with Article 1, Section 7. *See id.* at 442.

[30] *Id* at 433.

[31] *Id.*

[32] *Id.* at 434 (quoting *Association of Data Processing Service Orgs.*, 397 US 150, 153 (1970)).

[33] *Id.*

[34] *Id.* at 435.

[35] 553 F.2d 190 (D.C. Cir. 1977).

[36] 617 F.2d 697 (D.C. Cir. 1979), *vacated and remanded, Goldwater v. Carter*, 444 US 996 (1979).

[37] *Id.* at 204.

[38] *Id.* at 208 (internal quotation marks omitted).

[39] *Id.* at 211.

[40] *Id.* at 213 (stating that "[t]o constitute injury in fact, the alleged harm must be 'specific … and objective'; appellant'sclaims regarding effectiveness are neither.") (quoting Laird v. Tatum, 408 US 1, 14 (1972)).

[41] 617 F.2d 697 (D.C. Cir. 1979), *vacated and remanded*, *Goldwater v. Carter*, 444 US 996 (1979).

[42] *Id.* at 702 (citations omitted).

[43] *Id.*

[44] 656 F.2d 873 (D.C. Cir. 1981), *cert. denied*, 454 US 1082 (1981).

[45] *See id.* at 881.

[46] See *id.*

[47] *Id.* at 881; *see also Moore v. US House of Representatives*, 733 F.2d 946, 956 (D.C. Cir. 1984) *cert. denied*, 469 US 1106 (1985) (stating that "Congressional actions pose a real danger of misuse of the courts by members of Congress whose actual dispute is with their fellow legislators").

[48] *See, e.g., Moore*, 753 F.2d at 956; *Compare American Fed'n of Gov't Employees v. Pierce*, 697 F.2d 303 (D.C. Cir.1982) (granting standing to Member of Congress based on Kennedy); *Vander Jagt v. O'Neill*, 699 F.2d 1166 (D.C. Cir1982) (granting standing, but dismissing based on remedial discretion); *Moore v. House of Representatives*, 733 F.2d946 (D.C. Cir. 1984) (granting standing, but dismissing based on remedial discretion); *Barnes v. Kline*, 759 F.2d 21 (D.C. Cir. 1984) (granting Representative standing, not dismissing due to lack of legislative remedies, and reaching themerits); *Synar v. United States*, 626 F.Supp 1374 (D.D.C. 1986) (three-judge court) (granting standing to Members ofCongress, not dismissing based on equitable discretion because act in question authorized suit); *Boehner v. Anderson*,30 F.3d 156 (D.C. Cir. 1994) (granting standing) *with Crockett v. Reagan*, 720 F.2d 1355 (D.C. Cir. 1983) (affirmingdismissal of Representative's claim based on equitable discretion); *United Presbyterian Church v. Reagan*, 738 F.2d1375 (D.C. Cir. 1984) (dismissing for lack of standing); *Southern Christian Leadership Conference v. Kelley*, 747 F.2d777 (D.C. Cir. 1984) (denying standing to Senator); Gregg v. Barrett, 771 F.2d 539 (D.C. Cir. 1985) (dismissingRepresentative's claim based on equitable discretion); *Melcher v. Federal Open Mkt. Comm.*, 836 F.2d 561 (D.C. Cir.1987) (dismissing based on equitable discretion); *Humphrey v. Baker*, 848 F.2d 211 (D.C. Cir 1988) (dismissing basedon equitable discretion); *Doman v. United States Secretary of Defense*, 851 F.2d 450 (D.C. Cir. 1988) (dismissingbased on equitable discretion or lack of standing); *Michel v. Anderson*, 14 F.3d 623 (D.C. Cir. 1994) (not fullyexploring legislator standing and equitable discretion because of the presence of private plaintiffs); *Skaggs v. Carle*,110 F.3d 831 (D.C. Cir. 1997) (concluding plaintiffs lack standing because injury is "hypothetical").

[49] 733 F.2d at 951.

[50] 521 US 811 (1997).

[51] Line Item Veto Act of 1996, P.L. 104-130, § 692(a)(1), 110 Stat. 1200 (1996).

[52] *Id.* at 818-20.

[53] *Id.* at 830 n.11.

[54] 395 US 486 (1969); *see also supra*, notes 19 and 20 and accompanying text.

[55] Justice Souter's concurring opinion seemed to attach less importance than the majority to the distinction between personal and official injury, but he nevertheless agreed with the majority that the plaintiffs lacked standing. *See id.* at 831. Justice Breyer, however, dissented, arguing that there is no absolute constitutional distinction between cases involving a "personal" harm and those involving an "official" harm, and would have granted standing. *See id.* at 841-843. Unlike the majority, which viewed injury to a legislator's voting power as an official injury, Justice Stevens, in his dissenting opinion, asserted that a legislator has a personal interest in the ability to vote, and stated that deprivation of the right to vote would be a sufficient injury to establish standing. *See id.* at 837 n.2

[56] *See Chenoweth v. Clinton*, 997 F. Supp. 36, 38-39 (D.D.C. 1998), *aff'd*, 181 F.3d 112 (D.C.Cir. 1999) (holding that personal injury claims are more likely to result in a grant of standing, but mere institutional injury is sufficient under *Raines*); *see also Planned Parenthood v. Ehlmann*, 137 F.3d 573, 577-78 ($8^{th}$ Cir. 1998)(addressing the standing of state legislators).

[57] *See Raines*, 521 US at 826. Therefore, *Raines* did not address the question of whether *Coleman* would warrant granting standing in a suit by federal legislators even though such an action raises separation of powers concerns not present in *Coleman*. *See id.* at 824, n.8.

[58] *Raines*, 521 US at 289.

[59] *See id.*, at 822-24; *see also Moore v. US House of Representatives*, 733 F.2d 946, 951-52 (D.C. Cir. 1984), *cert. denied*, 469 US 1106 (1985).

[60] *See Raines*, 521 US at 820-21.

[61] *See* WRIGHT, MILLER, AND COOPER, FEDERAL PRACTICE AND PROCEDURE § 3531.11, at 1 (2001 Supp.) [hereinafter Wright & Miller].

[62] *See Raines*, 521 US at 824.

[63] See WRIGHT & MILLER, *supra* note 61, at 1.

[64] *See, e.g., Coleman v. Miller*, 307 US 433 (1939); *see also Kennedy v. Sampson*, 511 F.2d 430 (D.C. Cir. 1974); *Riegle v. Federal Open Market Committee*, 656 F.2d 879, n. 6 (D.C. Cir. 1981), *cert. denied*, 454 US 1082 (1981).

[65] 181 F.3d 112 (D.C. Cir. 1999).

[66] *Id.* at 113 (internal quotation marks omitted).

[67] *See id.*

[68] *Id.*

[69] 203 F.3d 19 (D.C. Cir. 2000), *cert. denied*, 531 US 815 (2000).

[70] *Id.* at 19-20.

[71] *Id.* at 22.

[72] *Id.* at 22-23.

[73] The National Energy Policy Development Group was created by President Bush via presidential memorandum and tasked with developing a national energy policy "designed to help the private sector, and government at all levels, promote dependable, affordable, and environmentally sound production and distribution of energy for the future." The President's memorandum directed the Vice President to serve as chair, with membership extended to the Secretary of the Treasury, the Secretary of the Interior, the Secretary of Agriculture, the Secretary of Commerce, the Secretary of Transportation, the Secretary of Energy, as well as several other federal officers. The memorandum also directed the Department of Energy to make funds available to the NEPDG to cover the costs of support staff.

[74] Letter from Reps. Waxman and Dingell to GAO, April 19, 2001.

[75] For detailed chronologies of interactions between the Office of the Vice President and GAO, *see* Letter from VicePresident Cheney to the House of Representatives, August 2, 2001; *see also* GAO Report on Vice President Cheney'sRefusal to Release Records, August 17, 2001.

[76] GAO Demand Letter to Vice President Cheney, July 18, 2001.

[77] 521 US 811 (1997).

[78] *Walker*, 230 F.Supp.2d at 65 (quoting *Raines*, 521 US at 819).

[79] *Id.* at 66.

[80] *Id.* at 66.

[81] *Id.* at 67 (quoting *Warth v. Seldin*, 422 US 490, 499 (1975)).

[82] *Id.* at 68. The court noted several other factors that contributed to its holding. In particular, the court found it significant that Congress had an "alternate remedy" to cure its alleged injury, in that it could issue a subpoena for the information. *Id.* at 30. Also, the court gave some weight to the fact that while its decision prevented the Comptroller General from gaining access to the NEPDG documents, private parties were seeking similar information in other suits. *See id.* at 31 n.14. Finally, the court was further influenced by the fact that there was no precedent for a suit by a Comptroller General for access to executive branch records, and that no court has "ever ordered the Executive Branch to produce a document to Congress or its agents." *Id.* at 32-33.

[83] *Id.* at 69.

[84] *Id.* at 69-70.

[85] *Id.* at 69 (quoting *Allen v. Wright*, 468 US 737, 752 (1984)).
[86] 558 F.Supp.2d 53 (D.D.C. 2008).
[87] *Id.* at 71 (emphasis in original).
[88] *Id.*
[89] US CONST., Art. III, § 2, cl. 1.
[90] *See* ERWIN CHEMERINSKY, FEDERAL JURISDICTION, 264 (3d Ed. 1999) (citing *Osborn v. Bank of the United States*, 22 US (9 Wheat.) 738 (1824)).
[91] *See* Act of Mar. 3, 1875, ch. 137, 18 Stat. 470 (codified as amended at 28 USC. § 1331 (2000) (stating that "[t]he district courts shall have original jurisdiction of all civil actions arising under the Constitution, laws, or treaties of the United States.").
[92] *Verlinden B.V. v. Central Bank of Nigeria*, 461 US 480, 494-95 (1983) (internal quotation marks and citationsomitted).
[93] 277 US 376 (1928).
[94] *Id.* at 378 (citing S.Res. 195, 69th Cong., 1st Sess. (1926)).
[95] *Id.* at 378-79.
[96] *Id.* at 387.
[97] *Id.* at 388 (citing *McGrain v. Daugherty*, 273 US 135, 160-174 (1927)).
[98] *Id.* (citing R.S. §§ 101-104, (codified as amended at 2 USC. §§ 192, 194 (2000))).
[99] *Id.* at 389.100 *Id.*
[100] *Id.*
[101] *Committee on the Judiciary, US House of Representatives v. Miers*, 558 F.Supp.2d 53 (D.D.C. 2008); *see alsosupra* notes 86-88 and accompanying text.
[102] 366 F. Supp. 51 (D.D.C. 1973).
[103] *See* S.Res. 60, 93d Cong. (1973).
[104] *Id.* at 61.
[105] *Id.* at 55-61.
[106] 28 USC. § 1331 (1970).
[107] *Senate Select Committee*, 366 F. Supp. at 59 (citing *Holt v. Indiana Mfg. Co.*, 176 US 68 (1900); *United States v. Sayward*, 160 US 493 (1895)) (emphasis in original).
[108] *Id.* at 61 (stating that "[e]ach of plaintiffs' assertions ... regarding the amount-in-controversy are legally inadequate,and finding no possible valuation of the matter which satisfies the $10,000 minimum, the Court cannot assertjurisdiction by virtue of § 1331.").
[109] *United States v. American Telephone & Telegraph Co.*, 551 F.2d 384, 389 (D.C. Cir. 1976) (citing *Committee for GIRights v. Callaway*, 518 F.2d 466, 472-73 (1975)); *see also Greer v. Spock*, 424 US 828 (1976)
[110] *See* P.L. 96-486 § 2(a), 94 Stat. 2369 (1980).
[111] *Waxman v. Thompson*, No. 04-3467, slip op. (C.D. Cal. July 24, 2006).
[112] 567 F.2d 121.
[113] *Waxman v. Thompson*, No. 04-3467, slip op. at 29 (C.D. Cal. July 24, 2006) (emphasis added).
[114] *United States v. American Telephone & Telegraph Co.*, 551 F.2d 384, 385 (D.C. Cir. 1976).
[115] *Id.* at 386. The precise details of the delicate negotiations between the DOJ and the subcommittee are explained by the court, *see id.* at 386-88, and, therefore, will not be recounted here.
[116] *See* H.Res. 1420, 94th Cong. (1976); *see also* H.Rept. 94-1422, 94th Cong. (1976).
[117] *Id.*
[118] *Id.*
[119] *See* 122 CONG. REC. 27,865-866 (Aug. 26, 1976).
[120] *See United States v. American Telephone & Telegraph*, 419 F.Supp. 454, 458 (stating that "[t]he effect of anyinjunction entered by this Court enjoining the release of materials by AT&T to the Subcommittee would have the sameeffect as if this Court were to quash the Subcommittee's subpoena. In this sense the action is one against the power ofthe Subcommittee and should be treated as such, assuming that Representative Moss has authority to speak for theSubcommittee.").

[121] *See generally, Ashland Oil, Inc. v. FTC*, 548 F.2d 977 (D.C. Cir. 1976); *see also* H.R. 899, 94th Cong., 1st Sess.(1975); 121 CONG.REC. 41,707 (1976).

[122] *Ashland Oil, Inc. v. FTC*, 409 F.Supp. 297, 301 (D.D.C. 1976).

[123] *Ashland Oil*, 548 F.2d at 979.

[124] 589 F.2d 786 (5th Cir. 1979).

[125] The Subcommittee on Oversight and Investigations of the Committee on Interstate and Foreign Commerce, and the Subcommittee on SBA and SBIC Authority and General Small Business Problems of the Committee on Small Business. *See id.* at 788.

[126] *See In re Beef Industry Antitrust Litigation*, 457 F.Supp. 210, 212 (D.C.Tex. 1978) (stating that "the persons whom the Subcommittees have subpoenaed would not have possession of the subpoenaed documents but for the discovery rules of the Federal Courts. Congress by subpoenaing these documents is interfering with the processes of a Federal Court in an individual case.").

[127] *In Re Beef*, 589 F.2d at 789. 128 *Id.*

[129] *Id.*

[130] *Id.* at 790-91.

[131] *Id.* at 790.

[132] *Id.* at 791.

[133] *Waxman v. Thompson*, No. 04-3467, slip op. (C.D. Cal. July 24, 2006).

[134] *Id.* at 2.

[135] 5 USC. § 2954 (2000) (emphasis added).

[136] *Waxman v. Thompson*, No. 04-3467, slip op. at 21 (C.D. Cal. July 24, 2006).

[137] *Id.* at 21, n. 42.

[138] *Id.*

In: Jurisdiction ISBN: 978-1-62081-429-1
Editors: A. Stewart and D. Washington 

*Chapter 2*

# THE INTERPLAY OF BORDERS, TURF, CYBERSPACE, AND JURISDICTION: ISSUES CONFRONTING US LAW ENFORCEMENT*

***Kristin M. Finklea***

## SUMMARY

Savvy criminals constantly develop new techniques to target US persons, businesses, and interests. Individual criminals as well as broad criminal networks exploit geographic borders, criminal turf, cyberspace, and law enforcement jurisdiction to dodge law enforcement countermeasures. Further, the interplay of these realities can potentially encumber policing measures. In light of these interwoven realities, policy makers may question how to best design policies to help law enforcement combat ever-evolving criminal threats.

Criminals routinely take advantage of geographic borders. They thrive on their ability to illicitly cross borders, subvert border security regimens, and provide illegal products or services. Many crimes—particularly those of a cyber nature—have become increasingly transnational. While criminals may operate across geographic borders and jurisdictional boundaries, law

---

* This is an edited, reformatted and augmented version of the Congressional Research Service Publication, CRS Report for Congress R41927, dated July 19, 2011.

enforcement may not be able to do so with the same ease. Moreover, obstacles such as disparities between the legal regimens of nations (what is considered a crime in one country may not be in another) and differences in willingness to extradite suspected criminals can hamper prosecutions. The law enforcement community has, however, expanded its working relationships with both domestic and international agencies.

Globalization and technological innovation have fostered the expansion of both legitimate and criminal operations across physical borders as well as throughout cyberspace. Advanced, rapid communication systems have made it easier for criminals to carry out their operations remotely from their victims and members of their illicit networks. In the largely borderless cyber domain, criminals can rely on relative anonymity and a rather seamless environment to conduct illicit business. Further, in the rapidly evolving digital age, law enforcement may not have the technological capabilities to keep up with the pace of criminals.

Some criminal groups establish their own operational "borders" by defining and defending the "turf" or territories they control. Similarly, US law enforcement often remains constrained by its own notions of "turf"—partly defined in terms of competing agency-level priorities and jurisdictions. While some crimes are worked under the jurisdiction of a proprietary agency, others are not investigated under such clear lines. These investigative overlaps and a lack of data and information sharing can hinder law enforcement anti-crime efforts.

US law enforcement has, particularly since the terrorist attacks of September 11, 2001, increasingly relied on intelligence-led policing, enhanced interagency cooperation, and technological implementation to confront $21^{st}$ century crime.

For instance, enforcement agencies have used formal and informal interagency agreements as well as fusion centers and task forces to assimilate information and coordinate operations. Nonetheless, there have been notable impediments in implementing effective information sharing systems and relying on up-to-date technology.

Congress may question how it can leverage its legislative and oversight roles to bolster US law enforcement's abilities to confront modern-day crime. For instance, Congress may consider whether federal law enforcement has the existing authorities, technology, and resources—both monetary and manpower—to counter $21^{st}$ century criminals. Congress may also examine whether federal law enforcement is utilizing existing mechanisms to effectively coordinate investigations and share information.

# INTRODUCTION

Savvy criminals constantly develop new techniques to target US persons, businesses, and interests. Central to the evolution of modern-day crime are four broad operational realities—geographic borders, criminal turf, cyberspace, and law enforcement jurisdiction. Individual criminals as well as broad criminal networks exploit these realities and often leverage the unique characteristics of one against the other to dodge law enforcement countermeasures and efforts to disrupt illicit activity. Further, the *interplay* of these realities can potentially encumber policing measures. In light of these interwoven realities, policy makers may question how to best design policies to help law enforcement combat ever-evolving criminal threats.

In the first operational reality, criminals routinely take advantage of geographic lines. They thrive on their ability to illicitly cross borders and provide illegal products or services. Indeed, much criminal activity is predicated on the ability to subvert border security regimens, thus earning a premium from black market clients and customers. Drug trafficking organizations (DTOs), for example, have constructed increasingly sophisticated cross-border tunnels to smuggle illegal drugs from Mexico into the United States. And, smugglers and fraudsters ship counterfeit goods from overseas, flooding US markets with sham goods and depriving genuine manufacturers of profits.

The second reality is broadly related to the first. Some larger criminal groups even establish their own operational "borders" by defining and defending the "turf" or territories they control. These boundaries are not formally recognized by law enforcement authorities, but they have strong influence in the criminal underworld. In fact, much of the violence in Mexico along the US Southwest border revolves around rival DTOs clashing over territorial control.[1] The outlines of turf can cross borders at the national, state, and local levels, thus complicating policing efforts.

The third reality involves a largely borderless, virtual environment where criminals carry out illicit business. Criminals operate in the cyber world partly to circumvent more conventional, established constructs such as international borders. In the virtual realm, criminals can rely on relative anonymity and a rather seamless environment to conduct business. For instance, some criminals use electronic banking systems to quickly smuggle cash out of one nation and into another.

Finally, US law enforcement often remains constrained by geographic and legal boundaries or even its own notions of "turf"—partly defined in terms of competing agency-level priorities and jurisdictions. US officials have suggested that as criminals have evolved their operations, they have relied less on turf to conduct business;[2] the same evolution is unclear regarding US law enforcement. Law enforcement agencies, even while collaborating through means such as interagency agreements, task forces, and fusion centers, retain investigational jurisdiction over organizational boundaries may remain.[3]

In addition to challenges presented by each of these four operational realities individually, law enforcement faces hurdles presented by the overlap of any or all of the realities. Complicating this, policy changes in one reality—both administratively and legislatively—can impact criminal activity and law enforcement countermeasures in other realities. Policy makers have expressed interest in ensuring that law enforcement is keeping pace with 21st century criminals who threaten American society.[4]

Given that criminal investigations unfold in an environment of geographic borders, criminal turf, borderless cyberspace, and law enforcement jurisdictions, policy makers may question how to direct policy to best enable US law enforcement to target contemporary criminals. For instance, Congress may choose to examine whether law enforcement agencies are effectively coordinating their investigations through the use of interagency agreements, task forces, and fusion centers. Policy makers may also debate whether law enforcement has the existing legal authorities, technology, and resources—both financial and manpower—to counter 21st century criminals. One of the principal debates for policy makers may be whether, or how, to design policies that cut across multiple operational realities.

This report examines the four operational realities within which law enforcement and crime operate. It analyzes the challenges for US law enforcement in each of these realities individually and in selected cases where they overlap. The report also discusses how law enforcement has adapted to combat present-day criminals. Throughout, it raises questions regarding how Congress may leverage its legislative and oversight roles to help US law enforcement most effectively protect US persons, businesses, and interests.

## BOUNDARIES IN THE OPERATIONAL REALITIES

Physical and virtual boundaries play significant roles in both criminal activity and police work. In the physical world, recognized borders delineate the lines of municipal, state, and national authority. At their most basic level, legally defined geographic borders outline the sovereignty of these entities.

For example, at official crossings along the US border with Mexico, law enforcement presence helps to distinguish one nation from another. Between ports of entry, the US Customs and Border Protection (CBP) has deployed personnel, technology, and tactical infrastructure along the Southwest border to impede the illegal entry of vehicles and unauthorized persons. When it comes to criminal turf, the virtual realm, and law enforcement jurisdictions, the lines separating one authority—legitimate or illegitimate—from another often grow fuzzier. The following sections lay out discussions of borders, turf, cyberspace (the virtual world), and jurisdiction that help shape modern criminal activity as well as law enforcement counter efforts.

## Borders

As suggested, physical or geographic borders—whether they divide countries, states, or even neighbors' plots of land—are often recognized with relative ease. Frequently, there are signals indicating when one is entering or leaving a given geographic area. Road signs, for instance, may provide notice of crossing from one city, county, state, etc., to another. International border checkpoints can signal that one is entering or leaving a country. Along several portions of the Southwest border, a fence separates the United States from Mexico.[5] Such physical boundaries may aid in delineating the space within which a given set of rules applies.[6]

Nations have sovereign control over their countries and territories and may enforce the laws of their lands within those bounds. In the United States, the federal government is responsible for enforcing federal laws within the country, and each state is responsible for enforcing state laws within its physical borders. And, rules that hold in one state may not apply in a neighboring state with different laws. For example, stealing $400 worth of goods is considered felony theft in California, but a criminal needs to steal $1,000 worth of goods in neighboring Arizona for the crime to reach the felony theft threshold.[7] Similarly, laws that apply in certain states may not apply under federal law to the country as a whole.

Globalization, technological innovation, and heightened security concerns have complicated traditional understanding of borders. Business, for instance, has become increasingly borderless;[8] so, too, have criminal enterprises. Since the terrorist attacks of September 11, 2001, the United States has experienced an expanded tension between border protection concerns and free market ideals.[9] Open border regimens are encouraged by a desire for efficiently moving goods and services. However, security screenings and concerns over safety may slow down the transit of these items. Criminals may then capitalize on any weaknesses in border regimens to supply black market goods and services where there is a demand. In other words, border protection systems and enforcement efforts can have the unintended consequence of introducing inefficiencies to market systems. These inefficiencies can, in turn, present profitable opportunities for criminal networks.[10]

## Turf

Some criminals—such as drug cartels and street gangs—have established turf boundaries for their operations. These boundaries may or may not coincide with geographically and legally defined borders. Criminal turf often delineates a territory within which illegal entities carry out their operations. In the United States, street gang warfare has historically centered around the establishment and protection of turf.[11] Other criminal networks have used various means to establish operational turf as well.

For instance, in February 2011, 22 members of a violent, fraudulent document-trafficking organization (including the manager of the organization's US operations) were indicted for crimes including the use of "brutal violence to eliminate rivals, protect its turf and enforce discipline against its own members."[12] The organization, based in Mexico, has operations in 19 US cities and 11 states, selling counterfeit Resident Alien and Social Security cards to unauthorized immigrants. The suspects in this case allegedly protected the organization's turf by posing as customers looking to buy the counterfeit identification cards. The "customers" would then attack competitors when they met for a supposed sale. Victims' hands, feet, and mouths were bound, and they were beaten and threatened with death should they continue to operate on the organization's turf.[13]

Turf may be readily established in the real world, as criminals can rely upon the physical environment to establish territory. In the cyber world, however, it may appear to be difficult to establish virtual turf lines, but they exist nonetheless . For example, two Trojans,[14] believed to be based in Russia, engaged in a cyber turf battle in 2010. The two Trojans—ZeuS and its smaller competitor, SpyEye—would both steal online banking information. They would then transfer funds to money mules, or US residents with bank accounts, who would then move the money out of the United States. SpyEye challenged ZeuS by stealing information from ZeuS and then removing the

ZeuS toolkit from infected computers.[15] The turf war reportedly ended when the ZeuS Trojan was no longer maintained and its code was allegedly merged with that of SpyEye.[16]

## Cyberspace

As mentioned, the relatively clear borders and turf lines within the physical world are not replicated in the virtual realm. Of course, some distinct boundaries separate the physical and the cyber worlds; a keyboard, mouse, screen, and password can all mediate between these physical and virtual realms.[17] Within cyberspace, however, the notion of a border is much more nebulous.

This is, in part, because the same geographic borders that exist in the real world do not exist in the cyber world.[18]

High-speed internet communication has not only facilitated the growth of legitimate business, but it has bolstered criminals' abilities to operate in an environment where they can broaden their pool of potential targets and rapidly exploit their victims. Between 2000 and 2010, the estimated number of internet users grew from almost 361 million to nearly 2 billion—an increase of more than 444%.[19]

Frauds and schemes that were once conducted face-to-face can now be carried out remotely from across the country or even across the world. The United Nations Office on Drugs and Crime notes that cybercrime has "evolved from the mischievous one-upmanship of cybervandals to a range of profit-making criminal enterprises in a remarkably short time."[20] US policy makers, officials, and law enforcement have become increasingly concerned about the threats posed by criminals in the virtual world.[21]

Even cyberspace, though, has some boundaries—both technological and jurisdictional. Some web addresses, for instance, are country-specific, and the administration of those websites is controlled by particular nations. For instance, website addresses ending in ".us" indicate that the United States owns the server controlling the website, while those ending in ".au" indicate Australian control.[22] Another barrier in cyberspace may involve subscriptions or fee-based access to particular website content.

Certain businesses—news sites, journals, file sharing sites, and others—may require paid access. There are also legal parameters governing what private citizens or law enforcement can lawfully do online. Despite this, an enhanced sense of anonymity offered to actors in the cyber world may encourage illicit behavior.

Certain traditional crimes such as fraud and identity theft are increasingly being seen as typical cybercrimes. A primary difference between these lines in the cyber and physical worlds is the venue in which crimes are committed. It appears that many crimes considered cybercrimes could be considered traditional, or "real world," crimes if not for the virtual venue in which they occur. On one hand, the virtual world may be seen as a borderless *space* that provides criminals with relative anonymity and a place to operate. However, cyberspace can also be seen as a *tool* that criminals use to subvert borders. Due to the global nature of the internet and other rapid communication systems, crimes committed via or with the aid of the internet can quickly impact victims in multiple state and national jurisdictions.

Recent congressional testimony from a Department of Justice (DOJ) official indicated that most cybersecurity incidents are transnational in nature.[23] For instance, in May 2010, US law enforcement indicted three individuals, located in the United States, Ukraine, and Sweden, for their roles in an international scareware scam.[24] The alleged fraudsters led internet users in these countries to falsely believe that their computers had become infected with malware. They then enticed their victims into buying bogus scareware software products that they advertised would remedy the contaminated computers. In reality, the software had no effect, as the supposedly infected computers were not truly compromised. This scam resulted in over $100 million in total losses.

Transnational cases such as this may raise proprietary questions regarding case investigation and prosecution and may cause significant challenges for law enforcement moving forward with the case, as is discussed later in this report.

## Jurisdictional Lines

For legal purposes, jurisdictional boundaries have been drawn between nations, states, and other localities. Within these territories, various enforcement agencies are designated authority to administer justice. When crimes cross state boundaries in violation of federal law, the states may no longer have sole responsibility for criminal enforcement, and the federal government may claim jurisdiction.[25] Importantly, laws remain effective *primarily* within the territorial lines of a given jurisdiction. Criminals have long understood this phenomenon—and exploited it. For example, boosters in organized retail crime (ORC) rings[26] may travel across state lines to target various locations of a specific retail establishment in multiple states. They can steal goods from each location, taking just enough to remain under the felony theft level for a given state and thus avoid prosecution for felony theft. In May 2009, for instance, four New York residents were arrested in New Hampshire for allegedly stealing hair care products from pharmacies. Authorities reportedly found in the suspects' van maps indicating drugstore locations in several East Coast states.[27]

Jurisdictional lines exist not only within the United States, but internationally as well. The United States shares borders with Canada and Mexico, and on each side of these boundaries, sovereign nations govern. A perpetrator committing a crime in the United States may flee across the northern or southern borders (or to another country overseas) to a land where the United States no longer has legal jurisdiction.

In one case prosecuted by DOJ, a New Jersey man was convicted in 2005 for his role in a conspiracy to bring heroin to the United States from Colombia. Before he could be sentenced, he fled to Colombia until he was later caught and extradited to the United States in March 2009.[28]

In the United States, jurisdictional battles exist not only between federal and state law enforcement—where these fights may be complicated by federal/state concurrent jurisdiction over a case—but between federal law enforcement agencies themselves.

Several agencies have overlapping missions and jurisdictions over the types of cases they may prosecute. For instance, there have been turf disputes between the Federal Bureau of Investigation (FBI) and the Bureau of Alcohol, Tobacco, Firearms, and Explosives (ATF) over cigarette smuggling and explosives cases, among others;[29] between US Immigration and Customs Enforcement (ICE) and ATF over transnational firearms trafficking cases and firearms cases involving unauthorized immigrants;[30] and between ICE and the Drug Enforcement Administration (DEA) over transnational drug trafficking and other cases.[31]

For law enforcement, these struggles to establish programmatic scope may be equally prevalent in the physical and cyber worlds. In both domains, however, agencies can rely, in part, on authorized jurisdictional boundaries to stake claim to their operational turf. And, in the real world, law enforcement can also rely on geographic borders where those borders simultaneously designate jurisdictional lines.

## INTERPLAY OF BORDERS, TURF, CYBERSPACE, AND JURISDICTION SHAPING CRIME AND LAW ENFORCEMENT

As mentioned, many 21st century criminals exploit borders and cyberspace in their illicit activities, and they occasionally establish operational turf. In addition, as criminals may clash over their turf, law enforcement, too, can struggle over jurisdiction. Each of these realities presents unique opportunities for criminals and challenges to US law enforcement. Further, the intersection of these elements can potentially compound obstacles to counter-crime efforts.

As seen in Figure 1, criminals may operate alone or as part of an extensive network. Without regard for geographic borders or law enforcement jurisdictions, criminals may organize with one another and carry out their illicit activities. Likewise, their operational turf is unconstrained by these lines. Criminals also rely on constantly advancing technology and near anonymity in cyberspace to work both within and across borders and jurisdictions.

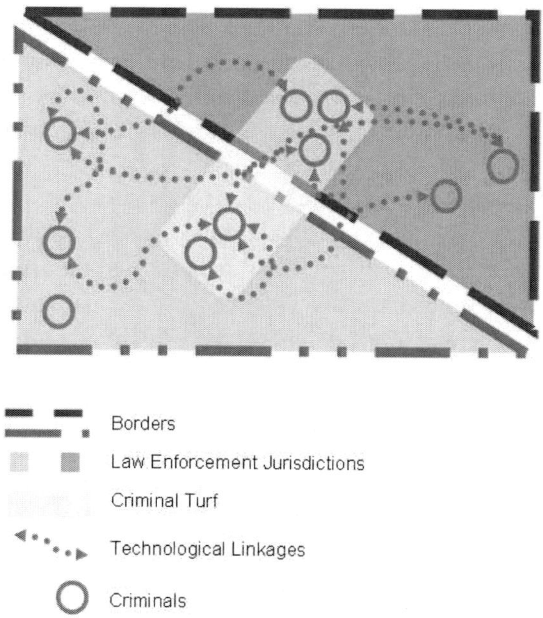


Source: CRS.

Figure 1. Conceptualization of the Operational Universe of Crime and Law Enforcement.

All the while, law enforcement jurisdiction is often constrained by boundaries—established by jurisdictions and otherwise. Even within a given jurisdictional boundary, multiple agencies may have investigative authority, contributing to possible disagreements over case leadership and control.

*Each of the four operational realities within which law enforcement and crime operate (borders, turf, cyberspace, and jurisdictions) also overlap. The following sections analyze selected areas of overlap, highlighting the modern-day opportunities for criminals and challenges to policing. In light of these interwoven realities, law enforcement and policy makers may question how to best design administrative and legislative policies to combat ever-evolving criminal threats.*

## Physical Borders and Jurisdictional Lines

One author has noted: "Criminal networks thrive on international mobility and their ability to take advantage of the opportunities that flow from the separation of marketplaces into sovereign states with borders."[32] Criminals are proactive, creative, and flexible. They are not constrained by jurisdiction in the same manner as law enforcement. They carry out their illicit activities in spite of geographic lines or jurisdictional boundaries. Criminals routinely move illicit products and proceeds across state and international boundaries.

Criminals have creatively circumvented both geographic borders and law enforcement jurisdictions. Mexican drug traffickers, for instance, utilize underground, cross-border tunnels— which have become increasingly prevalent and sophisticated—to smuggle drugs from Mexico into the United States. Simple "gopher hole" tunnels are dug on the Mexican side of the border, travel just below the surface, and pop out on the US side as close as 100 feet from the border. More advanced tunnels rely on existing infrastructure, such as storm drains or sewage systems. These systems may be shared by neighboring border cities such as the tunnel shared by Nogales, AZ, in the United States and Nogales, Sonora, in Mexico. Exploiting infrastructure allows smugglers to move drugs further than they could by digging tunnels alone. The most sophisticated tunnels can have rail, ventilation, and electrical systems. The most extensive of such tunnels discovered to date were found in January 2006 in Otay Mesa, CA. They stretched nearly three-quarters of a mile in length, traveled over 85 feet below the surface of the earth, and had lighting, ventilation, and groundwater drainage systems.[33] In November 2010, the San

Diego Tunnel Task Force[34] uncovered two similar tunnels running between Tijuana, Mexico, and Otay Mesa, CA.[35]

Traffickers have also used semi-submersible maritime vessels, ultralight aircraft,[36] and other means to move illicit products. Semi-submersible vessels are typically made of fiberglass, can travel up to 2,000 miles with multi-ton shipments of drugs—primarily Colombian cocaine—and are difficult to detect from the air.[37] The US Coast Guard has indicated that over 25% of the cocaine eventually destined for the United States is moved during part of its journey via semi-submersible vessels.[38] Mexican drug traffickers have increasingly used ultralight aircraft to smuggle drugs across the Southwest border. These small planes can fly as low as tree level and are not easily detected. Some traffickers land the ultralights on the US side of the border to pass off drug loads to distributors. Others attach drop baskets[39] to release packages of drugs that will fall to the ground when a lever in the aircraft is activated. These packages are then picked up and distributed by local traffickers or gangs. In FY2010, border authorities reported 228 ultralight incursions from Mexico into the United States—nearly double the number reported from FY2009.[40]

Smugglers and traffickers are constantly innovating means to circumvent borders and supply their products to areas where there is demand. In January 2010, smugglers along the Southwest border were intercepted in Mexico as they prepared a catapult device equipped to fling 4.4-pound packages of marijuana over the fence along the international border between Mexico and the United States.[41] While the attempt was unsuccessful—the drugs and catapult were both seized by authorities—this highlights criminal will to overcome physical, legal, and other barriers to generating profit. In another instance, in April 2010, smugglers used a portable folding ramp mounted on a truck to allow vehicles to drive over the international border fence. US Border Patrol agents spotted a vehicle that had used this ramp and seized 1,000 pounds of marijuana after the suspects abandoned their vehicle and fled back to Mexico.[42]

While many scholars believe that borders present opportunities for criminals, others have noted challenges. Criminals may be able to establish roots in new territory if there "is the presence of a demand for criminal protection in the new place. The presence of large illegal markets, booms in construction, an export-oriented economy, incentives to create cartel agreements, or the inability of the state to settle legal disputes quickly and effectively usually generate such a demand."[43] In fact, criminal organizations may expand into new territories by force rather than by choice. They may be moving to escape criminal infighting, turf battles, or effective law enforcement.[44]

### *Challenges for US Law Enforcement*

While criminals may operate across jurisdictional boundaries, law enforcement cannot. As mentioned, jurisdictional lines generally follow territorial lines, and US federal law enforcement may investigate and prosecute qualifying federal crimes within the territorial confines of the United States. For a given crime, federal law enforcement may be able to pursue an investigation provided that the criminal act, criminal actors, and victims are all within the United States. However, many crimes—particularly those of the cyber nature—have become increasingly transnational. While Congress has provided federal law enforcement extraterritorial jurisdiction for certain crimes, this does not necessarily clear law enforcement's path to engage in such investigations.[45]

Perhaps an alleged criminal committed a crime within the United States and then fled the country to evade prosecution. Or, perhaps a criminal targeted US persons, businesses, or interests from outside US territorial bounds. The United States may have to rely on other countries' law enforcement to assist in a criminal investigation or to help extradite suspected criminals to face prosecution in the United States. One such barrier to investigation and prosecution exists when the United States does not have an extradition or legal assistance arrangement with the country in which a fugitive has found haven.[46] Even if there is an extradition treaty, however, extradition can be complicated for a number of reasons. For one, an illegal action in one country may not be prohibited in another.[47] This could contribute to one country's reluctance to work with another or to turn over a suspect for prosecution. In the United States, for example, creating, possessing, and distributing child pornography are illegal; this is not the case, however, in a number of other countries. A 2006 study by the International Center for Missing and Exploited Children found that of 184 International Criminal Police Organization (INTERPOL) member countries, 95 countries had no laws criminalizing child pornography.[48]

The disparity between countries' cybercrime laws has been cited as another obstacle to investigations. Law enforcement has used the investigation of the "Love Bug," or "I Love You," computer virus as a prominent example of this barrier.[49] This virus was unleashed in the Philippines, and it attacked computers worldwide, including in Asia, Europe, Australia, and the United States. The creator of the virus, although arrested, was not charged with a crime because Philippine law at the time was not sufficient to address hacking and computer crimes.[50]

In addition to the challenges posed by investigating transnational criminals, impediments exist for US law enforcement in combating criminals crossing boundaries within the territorial United States. The prevention and control of domestic crime has traditionally been a responsibility of state and local governments, with the federal government playing more of a supportive role. However, between the mid-1980s and mid-1990s, federal law enforcement agencies saw an expansion of their role in fighting domestic crime as Congress began to add more crimes to the federal criminal code that were previously under the sole jurisdiction of state and local governments. While the federalization of crimes has increased, criminals can commit any number of crimes domestically that are investigated primarily under the purview of state and local law enforcement.[51]

Organized retail crime (ORC), for example, is often multi-jurisdictional. Retail criminals may operate freely across state lines, stealing just enough merchandise to remain under the major theft limit. Theft laws vary from state to state regarding the monetary threshold that constitutes major theft. There is currently no federal law specifically prohibiting organized retail crime as such, but there are provisions in the law that federal law enforcement uses to bring forth cases against ORC rings.[52] For crimes such as ORC that frequently cross borders, Congress has debated whether current law should be amended to provide provisions specifically criminalizing this activity. In this debate surrounding ORC, for instance, proponents of such legislation argue that criminalizing ORC may benefit law enforcement in several ways, including (1) illuminating the growing problem of ORC and (2) providing a statutory framework for tracking ORC case data rather than lumping these cases into other categories for statistical purposes. Opponents of legislation criminalizing ORC argue that already-existing statutes allow for effective investigation and prosecution of ORC and that creating a separate provision for ORC would be redundant. Indeed, representatives from federal law enforcement agencies have provided congressional testimony indicating that they have sufficient laws and procedural tools to investigate ORC.[53]

This highlights a larger federal debate regarding the federalization of offenses. In light of increasingly trans-border crimes, Congress may be faced with deciding whether these offenses are best criminalized at the state or federal level. One factor that may strongly influence this debate is whether state and local law enforcement agencies are equipped with the needed tools and authorities to keep up with savvy criminals who are constantly devising new means to profit and evade the law. One alternative to federalizing offenses is to provide state and local law enforcement with assistance—monetary, manpower, or technological. Congress has provided such assistance through funding grant programs such as the Community Oriented Policing Services (COPS) grant program[54] and the Edward Byrne Memorial Justice Assistance Grant (JAG) program.[55] Through these programs, state and local law enforcement assistance is available for a variety of purpose areas. Yet another option that Congress may consider is incentivizing federal, state, and local law enforcement coordination and information sharing through the participation in task forces and fusion centers. The issue of law enforcement coordination is discussed further in the section "Interagency Cooperation and Information Sharing."

## Cyberspace and Advancing Technologies

Globalization and technological innovation have fostered the expansion of criminal (and legitimate) operations across physical borders as well as throughout cyberspace. Advanced, rapid communication systems have made it easier for criminals to operate remotely not only from other members of their illicit networks, but from their victims as well.

### *Cross-Border Criminal Networks*

Criminal organizations have evolved to be more networked and cellular than their hierarchical predecessors.[56] Criminals operating as part of a network no longer need to live in the same city, state, or even country as one another. Various components of an organization may perform specific roles that need not be carried out in the same locality in which other members of the illicit network operate. As criminals take on more specialized roles, organizations may outsource portions of their operations to specialists. Specialists can be incorporated into a criminal scheme from all corners of the globe, and opportunistic networks may form around specific schemes. According to the US Secret Service (USSS), "more exclusive online groups [of criminals] count among their members professional criminals who have a decade or more of experience and extensive contacts in diverse criminal communities."[57] Web-based criminal forums, for instance, have global membership, many with "strong representation of members from Eastern Europe."[58] Some of these online forums act as business platforms where members of criminal communities can gather virtually to share and market their expertise.[59] One such forum was known as CarderPlanet, founded by Vladislav Horohorin, or "BadB." While CarderPlanet shut down after law enforcement arrested several high-level members,[60] Horohorin's criminal network "remains one of the most sophisticated organizations of online financial criminals in the world."[61]

As a byproduct of this organizational structure, one component of the network may have limited knowledge of the activities of other members of the network. Therefore, if one component is disrupted by law enforcement, other components of the network may be shielded by the loose organizational structure. While this may protect an organization from being wholly dismantled, it can potentially limit information sharing *within* an organization. This can subsequently stunt the sharing of key communications necessary for organizational learning and growth.[62] Indirectly, the cellular, networked structures that criminals have adapted and that, in part, allow them to more effectively operate across borders can hinder their internal operations and potential growth.

This phenomenon is not exclusive to criminal organizations, however. While there has been a trend towards increased information sharing in the law enforcement community—particularly since the terrorist attacks of September 11, 2001—compartmentalization still exists.[63] Agencies have adopted more intelligence-led investigations, but they still compartmentalize their operations and restrict information on a need-to-know basis.[64] In this fashion, they also put up barriers to potential organizational growth and learning. Some have suggested that while criminals and police both compartmentalize information, the means and speed with which they ultimately share information may differ. One scholar has analyzed this phenomenon in the context of smuggling networks, noting that they "often process information, make decisions, coordinate behavior, and change practices faster than the cumbersome bureaucracies that confront them."[65]

### *Trans-border Victimization*

Not only do criminals operate and network with one another across borders, but criminals (both individuals and organizations) often target victims without regard for borders. According to the Internet Crime Complaint Center (IC3),[66] of those reported scams and frauds from 2010 where the locations of the victim and perpetrator were both known, a minority of cases involved victims and perpetrators in the same state.[67] For instance, in California (the state with the largest proportion of victims and perpetrators reportedly in the same state), 39.1% of cases with known location information indicated that the victim and perpetrator were both located in California. Anonymity in the cyber world helps criminals operate with relative freedom. In addition, criminals may operate under numerous identities—actual, stolen, or cyber—that can link them to different parts of the world, confounding victims and law enforcement alike.

Modern criminals can readily leverage technology to victimize targets across borders. They can rely upon botnets,[68] for instance, to electronically target victims throughout borderless cyberspace. Simultaneously, the criminals themselves need not cross a single border. The Coreflood botnet, for one, has infected over 2.3 million computers around the world—almost 1.9 million of which are located in the United States.[69] This botnet, or virus, is a malicious keylogging program that records users' keystrokes and transmits the data to cyber thieves, who can use this data to steal personal and financial information. Compromised US businesses suffering financial losses from the botnet range from real estate and investment companies to law firms and defense contractors. The FBI has filed a complaint against 13 "John Doe" defendants believed to have engaged in wire fraud, bank fraud, and illegal interception of electronic communications in connection with the Coreflood botnet.[70] It is unknown whether authorities have determined the exact identities or locations of these alleged criminals, but they are believed to be foreign nationals.[71] Notably, authorities in the United States and Estonia have seized servers that are believed to have current, or have had previous, control over the Coreflood botnet.[72]

Advance fee fraud (AFF) schemes have, even before the proliferation of the internet, been used to swindle victims across borders. The internet has only hastened the speed with which these fraudsters can reach their targets and increased the number of potential victims. AFF scams often involve criminals sending unsolicited, or spam, e-mails that present an opportunity for a "lucky" individual to come into a large sum of money.[73] The letters promise the money will be disbursed once the victim sends a small cash payment, purportedly used to facilitate the transfer. Only, the large sum of money is never transferred to the victim. In one case from February 2011, the second of two Nigerian nationals was sentenced to nine years in prison for his role in an AFF scheme targeting US, European, and Australian individuals.[74] At least 18 people were duped out of over $9.5 million. The fraudsters posed as lawyers, bankers, and government officials who collected the "fees" that were advertised as necessary to secure the transfer of large sums of money to the victims. Of course, the victims never received their promised riches. The perpetrators were eventually arrested in the Netherlands (where they had been residing) and extradited to the United States.

The internet has also been used to perpetuate trans-border intellectual property rights (IPR) violations—one of the primary cybercrime concerns voiced by federal law enforcement and the Obama Administration.[75] Counterfeit and pirated goods harm legitimate businesses and consumers on several levels. This crime threatens competition and innovation, siphons profits deserved by the rightful manufacturer, and poses health risks to consumers. In June 2011, a Chinese national was sentenced for trafficking in counterfeit versions of the pharmaceutical weight-loss drug "Alli"—an over-the-counter weight-loss drug manufactured by GlaxoSmithKlein. The defendant reportedly shipped the products from China to a business partner in Texas for US distribution. The FDA had issued public alerts about this as well as other supposed weight-loss products.[76] The warnings indicated that the counterfeit drugs were being imported from China and that the "counterfeit version [of Alli] did not contain orlistat, the active ingredient in its product. Instead, the counterfeit product contained the controlled substance sibutramine." One consumer was even reported to have suffered a mild stroke after consuming the counterfeit product.[77] Over the course of the investigation, law enforcement purchased the counterfeit drug and traced the wired money used in the purchase of the counterfeit drug. They located the defendant in China and, posing as potential buyers of the drug, agreed to meet the defendant face-to-face. Law enforcement later met the defendant in Hawaii, where he was arrested. [78]

### *Barriers to Cyber Investigations*

Many of law enforcement's barriers in the cyber world have a technological dimension rather than being purely jurisdictional. Police agencies face challenges in identifying and prosecuting criminals who can operate under a variety of identities, including cyber identities that can be instantaneously altered, and who can conduct operations throughout the world without regard for borders (of which law enforcement is acutely aware). According to the FBI, "cyber criminals routinely change their nicknames, e-mails, digital currency accounts, and the ICQ [or instant messaging] numbers they use in forums. Not only do they change these accounts and identifying numbers, but they also use different combinations of the information in each forum they participate in."[79]

## Location of Crimes and Criminals

Cybercriminals often target victims in one or more different countries. Further, given the nature of the cyber world, crimes can be routed through servers in countries entirely separate from those where the perpetrators and victims are located. The Financial Action Task Force (FATF) has indicated that "it appears that the perpetrators take advantage of the near anonymity that can sometimes be achieved through internet communication on the internet, as well as the difficulty in following the path of communication links from one internet server to another."[80]

The Rustock botnet, for example, was a vast network of computers—estimated at over 1 million computers around the world—that sent malicious spam.[81] Reports indicate that this botnet may have been responsible for over half of worldwide spam at the end of 2010. "Command-andcontrol" machines, responsible for sending instructions to the other infected computers, were located primarily in the United States. Microsoft worked with the US Marshals Service and the Dutch High Tech Crime Unit in the Netherlands to dismantle the command-and-control structure.[82] In another case, from December 2010, DOJ arraigned a Russian national with the cyber identity "AKILL," who was the reported ringleader of the Mega-D botnet.[83] This botnet could send 10 billion e-mails daily. AKILL supposedly falsified the e-mail header information to disguise the e-mails' true origins. One technique to enhance anonymity used by botnet leaders, or botmasters, is to launder their internet traffic through a variety of intermediate internet hosts, protocols, and anonymous networks. Similar to money laundering, this traffic laundering makes it increasingly difficult for law enforcement to detect the source of the malicious botnet activity.[84]

## Same Crimes, Advanced Technologies

Criminals exploit rapidly evolving technology to stay ahead of law enforcement. Internet technology is used not only in the furtherance of cybercrimes, but in more traditional, real world crimes as well. According to Europol's 2011 Organized Crime Threat Assessment,

> Internet technology has now emerged as a key facilitator for the vast majority of offline organised crime activity. In addition to the high-tech crimes of cybercrime, payment card fraud, the distribution of child abuse material, and audio visual piracy, extensive use of the Internet now underpins illicit drug synthesis, extraction and distribution, the recruitment and marketing of victims of trafficking in human beings (THB), the facilitation of illegal immigration, the supply of counterfeit commodities, trafficking in endangered species,

> and many other criminal activities. It is also widely used as a secure communication and money laundering tool by criminal groups.[85]

While criminals are proactively searching for new techniques to accomplish the same crimes and generate money, law enforcement is reacting to criminals' activities. Take, for instance, advances in the movement of illegal drug trafficking proceeds across the US border with Mexico. While bulk cash smuggling has been an important means by which criminals have moved illegal profits from the United States into Mexico, traffickers have increasingly turned to stored-value cards to move money.

With these cards, criminals are able to avoid the reporting requirement under which they would have to declare any amount over $10,000 in cash moving across the border.[86] Current federal regulations regarding international transportation only apply to monetary instruments as defined under the Bank Secrecy Act (BSA).[87] Of note, a stored-value card is not currently considered a monetary instrument under current law. These transportation regulations indicate that

> Each person who physically transports, mails, or ships, or causes to be physically transported, mailed, or shipped, or attempts to physically transport, mail or ship, or attempts to cause to be physically transported, mailed or shipped, currency or other monetary instruments in an aggregate amount exceeding $10,000 at one time from the United States to any place outside the United States, or into the United States from any place outside the United States, shall make a report thereof. A person is deemed to have caused such transportation, mailing or shipping when he aids, abets, counsels, commands, procures, or requests it to be done by a financial institution or any other person.[88]

The Financial Crimes Enforcement Network (FinCEN)[89] has issued a notice of proposed rulemaking, intending to define "stored value" as "prepaid access" and to implement regulations regarding the recordkeeping and suspicious activity reporting requirements for prepaid access products and services.[90] The proposed rule would not, however, directly address whether stored value or prepaid access cards would be subject to current regulations regarding the international transportation of monetary instruments. Even if FinCEN were to implement regulations requiring individuals leaving the United States to declare stored value, the Government Accountability Office

(GAO) has identified several challenges that would remain.[91] These challenges relate to law enforcement's ability to detect the actual cards and to differentiate legitimate from illegitimate stored value on cards; travelers' abilities to remember the amount of stored value on any given card; and law enforcement's ability to determine where illegitimate stored value is physically held and subsequently freeze and seize the assets.

Aside from bulk cash smuggling and stored-value cards, traffickers move and launder money by using digital currency accounts, e-businesses that facilitate money transfers via the internet, online role-playing games or virtual worlds that enable the exchange of game-based currencies for real currency, and mobile banking wherein traffickers have remote access—via cell phones— to bank and credit card accounts as well as prepaid cards.[92]

**Technology Outpacing Law Enforcement**

Savvy criminals can evade law enforcement because they use, at times, technology and methods that are beyond the reach and expertise of law enforcement. In the rapidly evolving digital age, law enforcement may not have the capabilities to keep up with the pace of criminals. For instance, law enforcement specialists face mounting challenges in gathering information protected by sophisticated encryption.[93] Criminals can use data encryption software to mask electronic communications—sending information to undisclosed locations and individuals. While law enforcement may be able to intercept this data, they may not have the tools to crack the encryption and obtain valuable evidence.[94] This could potentially contribute to large amounts of data that can be collected but not analyzed.

The FBI has described a problem that results from a gap between investigative authority and capability. While law enforcement has the legal authority to conduct electronic surveillance and wiretaps, investigators may not be able to utilize these techniques if communications providers' technologies (or lack thereof) prevent law enforcement from implementing their legal authorities.[95] In essence, the FBI may be "'in the dark' by the loss of evidence, that [they] would be lawfully entitled to, due to advances in technology, antiquated ELSUR [electronic surveillance] laws, and or lack of resources, training, personnel."[96] As such, the FBI has created the "Going Dark" initiative (discussed later), which "is a National Electronic Surveillance Strategy which focuses on law enforcement's impending inability to conduct electronic surveillance on certain communications devices due to rapid changes in technology."[97] Not only can criminals' innovation and use of technology outpace law enforcement's investigations, but the relative costs to criminals and law enforcement appear to be unbalanced as well. Technology leveraged by criminals can be relatively low-cost.[98] In comparison, the costs to investigate these crimes—in terms of both financial and personnel resource costs—can be higher.

## Jurisdictional Battles

Establishing, maintaining, and expanding operational turf can all pose challenges to criminals. Criminals open themselves to increased exposure—to rival actors and law enforcement alike— when efforts to stake claim to and defend turf occur in the open. Criminals generally do not strive to publicize their illicit activities. In effect, this is a key element that separates criminals from terrorists. Criminals are often motivated by profit. They try to keep their activities under wraps without letting their identities be known. This anonymity increases the likelihood that they will be able to continue their activities without detection.

As noted, criminals operate with relative ease across borders. They have connections and trusted networks in different geographic areas. For instance, in order to facilitate the distribution and sale of drugs in the United States, Mexican DTOs have formed relationships with US street gangs, prison gangs, and outlaw motorcycle gangs.[99] While criminals may work through fluid trans-border alliances, law enforcement may not have parallel partnerships in each of the jurisdictional areas where criminal networks operate. Thus, criminals may be shielded from prosecution in jurisdictions with less robust police partnerships.

Nonetheless, turf battles between criminals continue to exist. These disputes are often seen in areas where gangs and other criminal networks are involved in trafficking and distributing illicit drugs. Researchers in Camden, NJ, studied violent crime near street corners with the presence of gangs (involved in drug distribution). Results of their research indicated that street corners with the presence of more than one gang have significantly more crime than those street corners with the presence of only one gang.[100] The scholars noted that these results are consistent with qualitative research suggesting that violence is likely in areas where territory is disputed.

Take, for example, the escalating drug trafficking-related violence in Mexico. Much of the violence had been a result of clashes between the drug trafficking organizations (DTOs) over territory within Mexico and key smuggling routes into the United States.[101] According to Mexican government official estimates, this violence has resulted in more than 34,500 deaths in Mexico since President Felipe Calderón took office in December 2006.[102] Targets of this violence most often include rival DTOs or affiliated gang members.[103] Increased violence and visibility of these battles have helped garner increased attention from both the Mexican and US governments, which have, in turn, elevated their determination and resources to combat the DTOs.[104]

Another way in which turf can be a barrier to criminals is that a heavy focus on turf can stunt criminals' profit if their activities are relegated to a particular turf. Focusing on a specific crime in a specific location may not prove to be the most profitable of business practices for criminals. Gangs, as mentioned, are notorious for violently defending the space in which they operate and controlling the activities that take place within given turf boundaries. While this has been standard practice, criminal gangs have modified this standard to expand their profitable activities both within and beyond their turf. According to the DEA, many "[g]angs have evolved from turf-oriented entities to profit-driven, organized criminal enterprises whose activities include not only retail drug distribution but also other aspects of the trade, including smuggling, transportation, and wholesale distribution."[105]

### *Evolution of Criminal Turf*

As discussed, to date, turf may have been more readily established in the physical world than in the cyber world—at least by criminals. Some have predicted, however, that this landscape may change in the coming years. In the cyber world, the evolution of operating systems may provide a wider variety of turf platforms on which criminals may operate. The number of Windows-alternative operating systems is increasing, and malicious code that some criminals use to compromise Windows, for instance, may not be compatible across operating systems. This diversification may contribute to establishing various platforms of cyber turf on which differing cyber gangs and criminal organizations may specialize their operations. This may contribute to what some have predicted—possible turf wars between hackers and groups of hackers.[106]

### *Law Enforcement and Operational Turf*

Just as territorial control impacts criminals, turf also influences law enforcement operations. While some crimes are investigated under the jurisdiction of a proprietary agency (e.g., the FBI is the lead federal agency responsible for terrorism investigations), other crimes are not investigated under such clear lines. For instance, various federal agencies, including the FBI, USSS, US Postal Inspection Service (USPIS), and ICE are involved in investigating identity theft.[107] Multiple agencies investigating a particular genre of crime can open the doors to investigative overlaps (and possible turf battles) as well as data challenges. According to GAO, a "lack of coordination can lead to confusion, frustration, and a waste of law enforcement resources; pose a risk to law enforcement personnel; and limit the overall effectiveness of the federal effort."[108]

## Investigative Overlaps

Jurisdictional battles between federal law enforcement agencies—particularly in areas of overlapping investigative authority—are not new phenomena. These battles have contributed, in part, to what some have characterized as inefficient information sharing. ATF's Project Gunrunner, for example, is one of various measures to reduce the illegal flow of weapons into Mexico. One purported cornerstone of Project Gunrunner is intelligence information sharing between federal, state, local, tribal, and international law enforcement partners.[109] It aims to disrupt the illegal flow of guns from the United States to Mexico, enhance US and Mexican law enforcement coordination, and train US and Mexican law enforcement officials to identify firearms traffickers. In November 2010, the DOJ Office of the Inspector General (OIG) issued a report on Project Gunrunner. The OIG report criticized Project Gunrunner, in part, because "ATF does not systematically and consistently exchange intelligence with its Mexican and some US partner agencies."[110] These domestic partner agencies include DEA and ICE. This lack of information sharing, and subsequent criticism, exist despite the presence of a Memorandum of Understanding (MOU) between ATF and ICE agreeing to enhance information sharing in cases of shared jurisdiction. It is unclear, however, whether the criticized lack of coordination arose from jurisdictional conflicts between partner agencies or from inefficient project planning and outreach to policing partners. Regardless, Project Gunrunner's inadequacies highlight the difficulties of sharing investigative information across agencies.

Another example of shared jurisdiction and inter-agency competition involves the National Cyber Investigative Joint Task Force (NCIJTF). In 2008, the FBI established the NCIJTF to coordinate information from 18 intelligence and law enforcement agencies. This task force was created to share information on all domestic cyber threat investigations.[111] An April 2011 DOJ OIG report indicated that "the NCIJTF was not always sharing information about cyber threats among the partner agencies participating in the NCIJTF" and that "task force members first attempted to determine the relevancy and importance of its information to another agency's operations before sharing that information with another agency."[112]

In essence, it appears that members were sharing information more on a need-to-know basis rather than automatically. In addition, the report indicated that during NCIJTF threat focus cell meetings, where agencies share new information regarding specific cyber threats, some agencies were asked to leave.

Recently, GAO released a study on law enforcement coordination within DOJ. Over one-third (37%) of DOJ agents from the FBI, DEA, ATF, and US Marshals interviewed by GAO indicated that they had experienced disagreements with other DOJ agencies regarding roles and responsibilities in an investigation.[113] Further, of those agents reporting disagreements, 78% indicated that these inter-agency disputes adversely impacted investigations. Also within the subset of agents reporting disagreements, 28% indicated that the source of the problem was a lack of information sharing from other agencies conducting similar investigations. The GAO study also suggests that the more agencies there are sharing jurisdiction on a particular investigative area, the less clear the agents may be regarding their agency's roles and responsibilities.[114] This lack of clarity may invite more turf battles and disputes that could in turn hamper an investigation.

Of note, not all investigative overlaps result in turf battles, and not all turf battles are ultimately detrimental to law enforcement efforts. Agencies can capitalize on shared jurisdiction and effectively pool their efforts, as is discussed in detail in the section "Interagency Cooperation and Information Sharing."

### Information and Data Sharing

When multiple agencies investigate a particular type of crime, a lack of centralized, compatible, comprehensive data may hamper their abilities to measure the true scope of a crime, share information, and coordinate investigations.

For instance, several federal agencies investigate and record information on bulk cash smuggling. These include the DEA through the National Seizure System at the El Paso Intelligence Center (EPIC), ICE through its Bulk Cash Smuggling Center, and the Department of the Treasury through the Treasury Enforcement Communications System database. Each of these databases is distinct from the others, and they are not set up to automatically share information. Of note, the Office of National Drug Control Policy (ONDCP) has recommended that increased information sharing among federal agencies—as well as between federal, state, and local law enforcement—could aid in investigations of DTOs involved in bulk cash smuggling.[115]

Similarly, there are multiple agencies gathering information on cybercrime and specific subsets of cybercrime. For example, there are various agencies collecting data on identity theft. The FBI partners with the National White Collar Crime Center to host the Internet Crime Complaint Center (IC3). The IC3 has a database of cybercrime complaints, including those regarding identity theft.

The Federal Trade Commission is another agency maintaining a database of consumer complaints on a range of frauds such as identity theft. ICE also collects this information through its Cyber Crime Center (C3), and the USPIS maintains information in its Financial Crimes Database.

The range of agencies and databases hosting information on identity theft can present challenges to law enforcement effectively combating the crime. Moreover, the President's Identity Theft Task Force noted that

> One barrier to more complete coordination is that identity theft information resides in multiple databases, even within individual law enforcement agencies. A single instance of identity theft may result in information being posted at federal, state, and local law enforcement agencies, credit reporting agencies, credit issuers, financial institutions, telecommunications companies, and regulatory agencies. This, in turn, leads to the inefficient "stove-piping" ofrelevant data and intelligence. Additionally, in many cases, agencies do not or cannot share information with other agencies, making it difficult to determine whether an identity theft complaint is related to a single incident or a series of incidents.[116]

Even when centralized databases, information sharing mechanisms, or directives are available, inter-agency coordination and sharing may not occur. For instance, DOJ has issued two MOUs in an attempt to clarify FBI and ATF roles in explosives investigations.[117]

The first MOU, in 2004, reportedly had ambiguous language regarding how to determine a lead agency in explosives investigations. In addition, DOJ, FBI, and ATF did not implement the outlined procedures regarding information sharing, database consolidation, training, and laboratory resources.[118]

A subsequent 2008 MOU reportedly had similar issues in that it did not clarify investigative jurisdiction.[119] DOJ's Office of the Inspector General (OIG) has indicated that despite two MOUs, FBI and ATF do not adequately coordinate their explosives investigations and continue to dispute which is the lead agency in a given investigation.[120] Further, as of 2009, the two agencies continued to maintain separate explosives-related databases despite instructions in the 2004 MOU directing their consolidation.[121] Jurisdictional battles impacting information sharing are not exclusive to federal law enforcement agencies.

Such discrepancies may exist between federal and state or local law enforcement, as well as between federal law enforcement and foreign counterparts. For example, multilateral information relating to drug, alien, and weapon smuggling is intended to be shared through EPIC.[122] EPIC is a fully coordinated, multi-agency tactical intelligence center supported by databases and resources from member agencies. Its online query capability consists of 33 federal databases, six commercial databases, and its own internal database. It operates a 24/7 watch program manned by special agents, investigative assistants, and intelligence analysts to provide timely tactical intelligence in support of field operations. In a June 2010 review of the El Paso Intelligence Center, DOJ's OIG indicated that the lack of an up-to-date agreement between EPIC and its member agencies has led to several coordination issues, including a lack of information sharing among agencies.[123]

Similar OIG critiques have been made of the National Gang Intelligence Center (NGIC). The NGIC coordinates intelligence information from federal, state, and local policing agencies. It supports law enforcement investigations by providing strategic and tactical analysis of intelligence.[124] In a November 2009 DOJ OIG review of DOJ's anti-gang intelligence and coordination centers (including NGIC), the OIG concluded that the NGIC had not created a gang information database, as had been directed by Congress.[125]

Further, the "NGIC is perceived as predominately an FBI organization, and it has not developed the capability to effectively share gang intelligence and information with other law enforcement organizations." It cannot be determined however, whether the coordination flaws were due to jurisdictional struggles between partner agencies or to a lack of information-sharing mechanisms in place. When exercising its oversight role, one issue Congress may wish to explore is whether existing MOUs and other inter-agency agreements regarding information sharing are being adequately formulated and implemented. Congress may also investigate the extent to which these agreements are being effectively overseen by applicable agency leadership.

# US LAW ENFORCEMENT EFFORTS TO OVERCOME BARRIERS

Modern-day criminals take advantage of geographic borders, criminal turf, cyberspace, and law enforcement jurisdictions. This has led law enforcement to transform their crime fighting efforts. For instance, the FBI has—particularly since September 11, 2001—relied more heavily on collaboration, information sharing, and technology.[126] The following sections outline how federal law enforcement has relied on interagency cooperation and technological implementation to confront 21st century crime.

## Interagency Cooperation and Information Sharing

As discussed, crimes—particularly those considered cybercrimes or that contain a cyber component—are increasingly trans-border and transnational. Further, criminal organizations are becoming less hierarchical and more networked in structure. These evolutions in the nature of crime and criminal organizations may require that law enforcement simultaneously become more nimble and networked in order to effectively counter the threats. Generally, law enforcement agencies and government entities charged with combating criminal networks are relatively hierarchical in comparison, and some experts have suggested that "hierarchies have a difficult time fighting networks."[127] This does not necessarily mean that it would be possible or even beneficial to make law enforcement and government entities less hierarchical. However, law enforcement adoption of networked practices (rather than actual structure) may better equip them to confront 21st century criminals.[128]

One such networked practice involves interagency coordination. Federal law enforcement has already taken steps to network with other federal, state, local, and international partners. This model has been used for decades to combat more traditional crime, and it has more recently been used to combat cybercrime. For instance, the FBI began embedding agents with international law enforcement partners in Romania in 2006 in order to target cyber criminals.[129] FBI collaboration has since been expanded to countries including Estonia, Ukraine, and the Netherlands.[130] These partnerships have proved beneficial in investigating and prosecuting transnational criminals. For example, law enforcement agencies including the FBI, USSS, Estonian Central Criminal Police, Netherlands Police Agency National Crime Squad High Tech

Crime Unit and the Netherlands National Public Prosecutor's Office, as well as the Hong Kong Police Force, all contributed to investigating a criminal network involved in hacking the RBS WorldPay computer network.[131] Five hackers have been indicted in the case. These individuals allegedly defeated the encryption used by RBS WorldPay to protect customer information associated with the payroll card processing system. Using counterfeit payroll debit cards—cards that allow employees to withdraw their regular salaries from ATMs—the hackers and their associates withdrew more than $9 million from over 2,100 ATMs across at least 280 cities around the globe—including in the United States, Russia, Ukraine, Estonia, Italy, Hong Kong, Japan, and Canada. Notably, the over $9 million loss occurred in under 12 hours.[132] In August 2010, Estonia extradited to the United States one of the principal leaders of the hacking ring, who has since been arraigned on charges of conspiracy to commit wire fraud, wire fraud, conspiracy to commit computer fraud, computer fraud, and aggravated identity theft.[133]

In another case, from June 2011, US, Colombian, and Italian law enforcement worked together to investigate "La Oficina de Envigado," a Colombian narcotics trafficking and money laundering network.[134] The organization—a vestige of the notorious Medellín Cartel—is based in Medellín, Colombia, but operates internationally, including in Massachusetts. Authorities seized 48 bank accounts in the United States. In addition, officials estimate that through the course of this operation, known as "Operation Fire and Ice," they seized over $200 million in cash, over 1,100 kilograms of cocaine, and 46 kilograms of heroin around the world.[135]

Federal law enforcement agencies may work with one another (and with their international counterparts), either informally or through formal agreements, to counter the transnational nature of crimes—both traditional and cyber. For example, the United States is a signatory to the United Nations Convention Against Transnational Organized Crime as well as the Council of Europe's Convention on Cybercrime and participates in the Group of 8 (G8)[136] High Tech Crime Subgroup, as discussed below.

### *United Nations Convention against Transnational Organized Crime*

The United Nations Convention Against Transnational Organized Crime is the primary international tool for combating organized crime.[137] In 2005, the United States ratified the convention as well as the companion protocols on trafficking in persons and smuggling of migrants. Among other provisions, the convention provides for greater law enforcement cooperation and mutual legal assistance across nations where there were no previous agreements for such assistance. The convention also requires signatories to criminalize certain offenses such as participation in an organized criminal group, money laundering, corruption, and obstruction of justice. It also requires the enhancement of training and technical assistance to combat transnational organized crime. By ratifying the convention in 2005, Congress took a step in working with foreign governments and law enforcement agencies to combat multi-national and multi-jurisdictional organized crime. Given the increasingly transnational nature of organized crime, this coordination with international organizations is seen as essential.[138]

### *Council of Europe Convention on Cybercrime*

The Council of Europe's Convention on Cybercrime was developed in 2001 to address several categories of crimes committed via the internet and other information networks.[139] It is the first international treaty on this issue, and its primary goal is to "pursue a common criminal policy aimed at the protection of society against cybercrime, especially by adopting appropriate legislation and fostering international co-operation." To date, 47 countries are signatories to the convention and 31 of these—including the United States—have ratified it.[140]

As mentioned, not all activities considered to be crimes in one country are also considered criminal acts in another. Further, there is not a harmonized view on what constitutes cyber or computer-related crime. Signatories to the convention, however, must define criminal offenses and sanctions under their domestic laws for four categories of computer-related crimes: security breaches such as hacking, illegal data interception, and system interferences that compromise network integrity and availability; fraud and forgery; child pornography; and copyright infringements. The convention also requires signatories to establish domestic procedures for detecting, investigating, and prosecuting computer crimes, as well as collecting electronic evidence of any criminal offense. It also requires that signatories engage in international cooperation "to the widest extent possible."

### *G8 High Tech Crime Subgroup*

DOJ is a key player in US participation in the G8 Subgroup on High Tech Crime. In 1996, the G8 created the Lyon group of experts on transnational organized crime. These experts developed Forty Recommendations to combat transnational organized crime. Subsequently, the G8 created various subgroups (one of which is a High Tech Crime subgroup) to address various crime-related issues.[141] The subgroup has created a Network for 24-Hour Points of

Contact for high tech crime. It has negotiated an action plan and a set of widely accepted principles to combat high tech crime. It has also created numerous best practices documents such as guides for securing computer networks, requesting international assistance, drafting legislation, and tracing networked communications across borders. The subgroup has assessed threats and the impact on law enforcement from new technology such as encryption as well as malicious internet activities such as viruses and worms. It has also sponsored training conferences for cybercrime agencies as well as conferences for law enforcement and industry on improved cooperation.[142]

***Interagency Agreements***

One mechanism that federal law enforcement agencies have used to try to minimize jurisdictional discrepancies and coordinate work is through interagency agreements and Memoranda of Understanding (MOUs). For instance, on June 30, 2009, ATF and ICE signed an MOU, citing a shared jurisdiction in combating criminal organizations engaging in violent crime and drug trafficking. The agencies agreed to involve one another in cases of shared jurisdiction and to enhance information sharing in such cases.[143] The DOJ OIG found that, despite this MOU,

> ATF and ICE do not work together effectively on investigations of firearms trafficking to Mexico, and therefore ATF's Project Gunrunner cases do not benefit from ICE's intelligence and prosecutorial options. ATF and ICE rarely conduct joint investigations of firearms trafficking to Mexico, do not consistently notify each other of their firearms trafficking cases, and do not consistently coordinate their investigative work with each other.[144]

The OIG attributed this lack of information sharing to both an unawareness of the MOU's existence as well as misunderstanding of its purpose.

ICE also shares an interagency cooperation agreement with the DEA that has been in effect since June 18, 2009. The agencies agree to share information through the DEA's Special Operations Division, the Organized Crime Drug Enforcement Task Force (OCDETF) program Fusion Center, and EPIC. The agreement also allows ICE to select agents for cross-designation by the DEA Administrator and permits these ICE agents to investigate narcotics smuggling with a clear nexus to the US border. It also provides procedures for deconfliction[145] and operational coordination in domestic and international cases.[146] On August 10, 2009, ICE and DOJ signed two MOUs to enhance information sharing at the OCDETF Fusion Center and the International Organized Crime Intelligence and Operations Center (IOC-2).[147] It is unknown, however, how well the agreements and MOUs between ICE and DEA as well as between ICE and DOJ have reduced any turf battles in their areas of overlapping jurisdiction.

### *Fusion Centers and Task Forces*

As modern law enforcement operations have become increasingly intelligence-led, agencies have come to rely heavily on fusion centers and task forces. According to DHS, fusion centers and task forces (with specific reference to Joint Terrorism Task Forces, or JTTFs) serve "distinct, but complementary roles."[148] Fusion centers have been defined as a "collaborative effort of two or more Federal, state, local, or tribal government agencies that combines resources, expertise, or information with the goal of maximizing the ability of such agencies to detect, prevent, investigate, apprehend, and respond to criminal or terrorist activity."[149] DHS has indicated that

> [F]usion centers serve as focal points within the state and local environment for the receipt, analysis, gathering, and sharing of threat-related information among federal and state, local, tribal, and territorial (SLTT) partners. They produce actionable intelligence for dissemination, which can aid other law enforcement organizations, including the JTTFs, in their investigative operations.[150]

While fusion centers are generally intelligence-based, law enforcement task forces appear to be generally operational in nature.[151] These multi-jurisdictional entities are established to counter a specific threat such as violent gangs[152] or online fraud.[153] The sections below discuss selected fusion centers and task forces.

### Fusion Center Model

The majority of fusion centers, located in states and major urban areas throughout the country, were created post-9/11, though interagency information sharing centers had been emerging since at least the 1990s.[154] One precursor to the formal fusion center concept is the High Intensity Drug Trafficking Area (HIDTA) program. The HIDTA program, originally authorized by the Anti-Drug Abuse Act of 1988 (P.L. 100-690),[155] provides assistance to federal, state, and local law enforcement operating in areas deemed as the most-impacted by drug trafficking. Each HIDTA is governed by a separate executive board comprised of about eight federal agencies and eight state or local agencies. The program's main goals are to

- assess regional drug threats;
- develop strategies focusing efforts on combating drug trafficking threats;
- create and fund initiatives to improve these strategies;
- facilitate coordination between federal, state, and local efforts; and
- produce efficient drug control efforts to reduce/eliminate the impact of drugtrafficking.[156]

The Director of the Office of National Drug Control Policy (ONDCP) has the authority to designate areas within the United States and its territories that are centers of illegal drug production, manufacturing, importation, or distribution as HIDTAs—of which there are currently 28.[157] The Southwest Border Region HIDTA, for example, includes portions of California, Arizona, New Mexico, and Texas. The HIDTA collects and shares intelligence and coordinates task forces composed of federal, state, and local agencies that target drug-trafficking operations along the border. In one case from June 2011, the Milwaukee, WI, HIDTA was involved in the indictments of 24 individuals involved in a drug trafficking and illegal gambling ring. Couriers in the network transported hundreds of pounds of marijuana from Seattle, WA, and Vancouver, BC, to Minnesota, Wisconsin, and Illinois, and transported bulk cash—about $1.3 million in proceeds from drug sales and illegal gambling—back to the Pacific Northwest.[158]

Several law enforcement fusion centers have been created to target criminal networks, including the Organized Crime Drug Enforcement Task Force (OCDETF) Fusion Center (OFC), the International Organized Crime Intelligence and Operations Center (IOC-2), the National Gang Intelligence Center (NGIC), and the El Paso Intelligence Center (EPIC). They are charged with consolidating and disseminating intelligence on various organized crime matters. For instance, the OFC assimilates information for the OCDETF Program, targeting major drug trafficking and money laundering organizations. The IOC-2—housed at the OFC—was created by DOJ in 2009 to bring together the FBI; ICE; DEA; IRS; ATF; USSS; USPIS; US Department of State, Bureau of Diplomatic Security; US Department of Labor, Office of the Inspector General; and DOJ's Criminal Division in partnership with the 94 US Attorneys' Offices and the US Department of the Treasury,

Office of Terrorism and Financial Intelligence. The IOC-2 is charged with analyzing and resolving information conflicts on a host of organized crime cases, not solely those that center on drug trafficking.

Despite successes using the fusion center model, not all fusion centers have been funded. While NGIC, EPIC, and the OFC have received funding, the IOC-2 has not. One issue that Congress may consider is whether such intelligence-sharing centers bolster federal law enforcement's abilities to combat networked, trans-border crime. If they are effective, Congress may debate whether increasing resources for existing centers would in turn increase law enforcement operations. Increased funding could boost law enforcement investigations in number and/or in quality. One question surrounding any increase in funding for investigations is whether enhanced investigative resources are balanced with complementary resources for prosecutions. If policy makers enable law enforcement to investigate a greater number of cases, they may chose to consider whether they are balancing investigative resources with prosecutorial resources.

With respect to the coordination of federal efforts to combat criminal networks, one non-legislative option that Congress may consider is enforcing its oversight over existing fusion centers. As mentioned, in June 2010, the DOJ Office of the Inspector General (OIG) issued a review of EPIC. The review suggested that, while EPIC's users value its products, EPIC could gain from fully developing the National Seizure System and coordinating the HIDTA program, consistently coordinating with intelligence organizations across the country, maintaining and analyzing current information from all available sources, and creating objective performance measures by which to evaluate its programs, among other things.[159] Before determining whether to increase, decrease, or maintain funding for existing fusion centers, policy makers may debate whether these centers have taken measures to most effectively obtain their respective goals. For instance, has EPIC taken measures to analyze current information from all its available resources or has the OFC effectively used its resources to pursue CPOT targets?

### Task Force Model

Federal law enforcement has increasingly relied on the task force model to coordinate investigations. One such task force is the Organized Crime Drug Enforcement Task Force (OCDETF) program. The OCDETF program targets—with the intent to disrupt and dismantle— major drug trafficking and money laundering organizations. Federal agencies that participate in the OCDETF Program include the DEA, FBI, ICE, ATF, US Marshals, Internal

Revenue Service (IRS), US Coast Guard (USCG), the 94 US Attorneys Offices (USAOs), and DOJ's Criminal and Tax Divisions. These federal agencies also collaborate with state and local law enforcement. The OCDETFs operate in nine regions around the country and target those organizations that have been identified on the Consolidated Priority Organization Targets (CPOT) List, which is the OCDETF filed 2,783 cases with the US Attorneys Offices.[161]

While OCDETFs operate throughout the country, Border Enforcement Security Taskforces (BESTs) operate along the northern and southern borders. The BEST initiative consists of a series of multi-agency investigative task forces, of which ICE is the lead agency.[162] They seek to identify, disrupt, and dismantle criminal organizations posing significant threats to border security along both borders. Other agency participants include CBP, DEA, ATF, FBI, USCG, and the US Attorneys Offices, and state and local law enforcement. The Mexican law enforcement agency Secretaria de Seguridad Publica is a partner along the Southwest border. On the northern border, Canadian law enforcement agencies like the Canada Border Services Agency, the Royal Canadian Mounted Police, the Ontario Provincial Police, the Niagara Regional Police Service, the Toronto Metropolitan Police, the Windsor Police Service, and the Amherstburg Police Service are active members. The Argentinean customs agency is part of the Miami BEST and the Colombian National Police is part of both the Miami and New York-New Jersey BESTs. Currently, there are 21 BESTs with locations around the United States and in Mexico. Each BEST concentrates on the prevalent threats in its area. On the southern border, for instance, this entails cross-border violence, weapons smuggling and trafficking, illegal drug and other contraband smuggling, money laundering and bulk cash smuggling, as well as human smuggling and trafficking.

Both policy makers and Administration officials have been concerned about financial fraud, particularly as the nation emerges from the most recent economic downturn. Because of these concerns, President Obama established a Financial Fraud Enforcement Task Force in November 2009.[163] The task force, chaired by the Attorney General, includes more than 20 federal agencies, the US Attorneys Offices, and state and local partners. It targets a range of financial crimes from mortgage fraud and identity theft to credit card fraud and Ponzi schemes. Recently, the task force was involved in investigating and prosecuting a husband and wife team for defrauding over 250 individuals of about $1.5 million through an internet fraud scheme. The couple advertised high-end kitchen appliances on e-Bay, though they were not licensed dealers of these products. When customers bought the advertised items, the team of perpetrators used this money to purchase luxury items and stocks and did not to deliver the merchandise.[164]

One task force centered around cyber threats is the National Cyber Investigative Joint Task Force (NCIJTF), led by the FBI. The NCIJTF includes 18 law enforcement and intelligence agencies that work together to counter a variety of cyber threats, including national security intrusions, criminal intrusions, online child pornography, intellectual property rights violations, and internet fraud.[165] Within this task force model, the FBI operates smaller Threat Focus Cells that center around specific types of cyber threat such as botnets.[166] The Botnet Focus Cell was instrumental in countering the Mariposa botnet. This botnet, also known as "Butterfly Bot," was an information-stealing botnet that infected up to 12 million computers around the world. Butterfly Bot stole passwords for websites and financial institutions as well as credit card and bank account information from computer users. The FBI investigated this case in collaboration with Spanish and Slovenian police, who arrested both users and the creator of the botnet.[167]

Policy makers may choose to evaluate whether the task force model is an effective means to share information and counter emerging threats. As illustrated, turf battles, even between agencies that have established working relationships, can hinder investigations. Agencies may be at odds over leadership in a given case. They may also share information on a "need to know" rather than a "need to share" basis.[168] Carefully protecting information, however, is not inherently problematic. The more people who have access to information, the greater the chances it can be leaked or intercepted by malicious actors. The need to keep investigative information from criminals' eyes is an incentive to keep intelligence information among as few individuals as possible.[169] Nonetheless, Congress may debate the appropriate level of information sharing within task forces as well as through other inter-agency forums.

### *Information Sharing Systems*

In addition to the benefits of operational collaboration and coordination, policy makers and law enforcement have cited the value of interagency information sharing. The push for information sharing has been more visible regarding the investigation of terrorism and related crimes than it has been for the investigation of more traditional crime. For instance, in the 2004 Intelligence Reform and Terrorism Prevention Act (P.L. 108-458), Congress mandated the creation of an Information Sharing Environment—commonly known as the "ISE."[170] Through this act, Congress also directed that the ISE provide and facilitate the means of sharing terrorism information among all appropriate federal, state, local, and tribal entities as well as the private sector through the use of policy guidelines and technologies. Congress has not directed the creation of such an information sharing environment for the investigation of more traditional crimes in either the real or cyber worlds.

While there is not a sole clearinghouse for information sharing on traditional criminal investigations, there are a number of databases that contain a given subset of information. These include the FBI's Law Enforcement Online, Automated Fingerprint Identification System, National Crime Information Center, National Data Exchange, and Violent Criminal Apprehension Program; ATF's Arson & Explosives National Repository and Bomb Arson Tracking System; and the High Intensity Drug Trafficking Area Deconfliction, among others.[171] Through a 2006 nationwide survey, the Justice Statistics and Research Association (JSRA) identified 266 information sharing systems (that were either in place or under development) spanning 35 states and Canada.[172] These systems share information about crime at the national, regional, state, and county levels. Of these systems, 10% were identified as sharing national-level data. When survey respondents recommended system improvements, the most common suggestion involved including additional agencies in the information sharing system.[173]

Databases have been established to coordinate information on specific types of crime. For instance, the National Identity Crimes Law Enforcement (NICLE) was established to coordinate information on identity theft and related crimes.[174] This network, organized and led by the US Attorney's Office for the Eastern District of Pennsylvania, consolidates information from local, state, and federal law enforcement agencies. Data in NICLE is available to nearly 100 law enforcement agencies through the Regional Information Sharing System Intranet (RISSNET).[175] The President's Identity Theft Task Force had recommended the establishment of a national database for law enforcement to consolidate information on identity theft.[176]

## Public/Private Partnerships

Law enforcement has recognized the benefits of working with private entities in order to gather information and enhance investigations. One such partnership is InfraGard, through which the FBI gathers information on cybercrimes and other cases.[177] InfraGard is an FBI partnership with businesses, academic institutions, and other law enforcement agencies. Through this program, the Bureau can collect and disseminate information to private sector entities as well as other law enforcement partners. The InfraGard program began as a means to share cybercrime information, but its mission has expanded to include other crimes and threats, particularly those involving critical infrastructure.[178] As of November 2009, InfraGard had more than 33,000 members across 87 US cities.[179]

Similar to InfraGard is the Domestic Security Alliance Council (DSAC).[180] DSAC is a security and intelligence-sharing initiative between the FBI, DHS, and the private sector, and the focus is on crimes impacting interstate commerce. These include computer intrusions, insider threats, fraud, theft of trade secrets, product tampering, and workplace violence. As of March 2011, DSAC had nearly 200 US private sector companies and organizations.

Another partnership—the Law Enforcement Retail Partnership Network (LERPnet)—has been established to combat organized retail crime.[181] In 2006, through the ViolenceAgainst Women and Department of Justice Reauthorization Act of 2005,[182] Congress directed the Attorney General and the FBI to establish a clearinghouse within the private sector for information sharing between retailers and law enforcement. The result was LERPnet. It began as a partnership between the FBI, ICE, various local police departments, individual retailers, and retail organizations including the Food Marketing Institute (FMI), National Retail Federation (NRF), and Retail Industry Leaders Association (RILA). As of January 2010, LERPnet has been linked with the FBI's Law Enforcement Online (LEO) system, providing federal and local law enforcement with a direct link to retail industry crime reports.

## Technology Implementation

Savvy criminals are constantly evolving their methods to stay paces ahead of law enforcement. They traverse through and around physical and cyber space, capitalizing on ever advancing technology to evade detection. In response, law enforcement has utilized an array of methods, from human intelligence to advanced technology to investigate these criminals.

As discussed, Mexican drug traffickers have dug subterranean tunnels to smuggle illicit drugs from Mexico into the United States. The United States employs various tunnel detection technologies such as ground penetrating radar (GPR) to locate and shut down these tunnels.[183] GPR is limited, however, by factors such as soil condition and tunnel diameter and depth. Law enforcement may also use sonic equipment to detect the sounds of digging and tunnel construction as well as seismic technologies to detect blasts that may be indicative of tunnel excavation. US officials have acknowledged that law enforcement currently does not have technology that is reliably able to detect the more sophisticated tunnels.[184] Rather, tunnels are more effectively discovered as a result of human intelligence and tips rather than technology. Indeed human intelligence, or HUMINT, "is the oldest method for collecting information, and until the technical revolution of the mid to late twentieth century, it was the primary source of intelligence. HUMINT is used mainly by the CIA [Central Intelligence Agency], the Department of State, the DoD [Department of Defense], and the FBI."[185] Further, the Interagency Threat Assessment and Coordination Group (ITACG) at the National Counterterrorism Center has indicated that "HUMINT can often collect information that is difficult or sometimes impossible to collect by other, more technical, means."[186]

As crime has transformed to involve more technology, law enforcement has moved to keep pace. Nonetheless, the FBI and others continue to recognize the value of human intelligence and confidential sources/informants. Reportedly, the FBI maintains over 15,000 such sources.[187] Even in cyber investigations, the FBI and other federal law enforcement agencies rely heavily on confidential sources. It has been estimated that "25% of hackers in the US may have been recruited by the federal authorities to be their eyes and ears."[188] Both the FBI and the USSS have had success in infiltrating the underground world of hackers, and hackers-turned-informants have worked not only with law enforcement, but with the military as well. For instance, in 2004 Adrian Lamo, a notorious hacker, pled guilty to hacking into *The New York Times*'s internal network containing personally identifiable information of *Times* contributors.[189] He also reportedly accessed the *Times*'s LexisNexis subscription account, creating fictitious usernames and conducting unauthorized searches. In 2010, Lamo was purportedly contacted by Bradley Manning, a US Army intelligence analyst who is alleged to have passed classified cables to Wikileaks. After Manning supposedly claimed responsibility for the leaks, Lamo reportedly turned Manning over to the Army and FBI.[190]

Despite the use of human intelligence, advances in technology, outmoded laws, and a lack of resources, training, and personnel can keep law enforcement "in the dark" as criminals evade detection.[191] Because of this very issue, the FBI has created the "Going Dark" initiative. This initiative is based on the premise that rapid changes in technology may impede the Bureau's ability to conduct electronic surveillance.[192] Law enforcement has indicated that while they have the legal authorities to do so, they may not have the technological capabilities.

Congress may debate how to best enable law enforcement to leverage their authorities and available technology to conduct necessary investigations while also protecting personal communications and privacy. One concern of privacy advocates is that enabling law enforcement to more easily obtain information from communications services providers could jeopardize individuals' privacy.[193] Some have suggested that "[a]lthough massive penetration into criminal communities may help curtail some unlawful activities, the invasive penetration into communities and the absolute control over whatever happens in the digital space amount to disruption of natural rights."[194] Policy makers may weigh whether the best means to aid federal law enforcement involve bolstering authorities to use encryption-breaking technologies, enhancing training of law enforcement personnel so they can best leverage existing authorities and technologies, or encouraging agencies to direct their manpower and financial resources to investigating cybercrimes, among other options.

## CONCLUSION

The operational realities of 21st century crime and policing present significant challenges to US policy makers. In particular, the interplay between borders, criminal turf, cyberspace, and law enforcement jurisdiction is such that policies directed toward countering crime in one reality will impact crime and law enforcement countermeasures in other realities. As such, Congress may choose to debate a host of legislative and oversight options to most effectively empower law enforcement.

Legislatively, Congress may consider whether law enforcement has the existing authorities, technology, and resources—both monetary and manpower—to counter 21st century criminals. For instance, given that many crimes are increasingly trans-border in nature, Congress may deliberate whether certain offenses are best criminalized at the state or federal level. If Congress determines that these crimes may be most effectively countered at the federal level, policy makers may consider expanding federal law enforcement's statutory authorities to investigate these offenses. Policy makers may also consider whether to direct existing or additional resources toward bolstering federal law enforcement agents' skills and abilities to counter modern day threats. For example, Congress may direct the allocation of agent resources toward combating more traditional, yet evolving, crimes such as financial fraud. Policy makers may also choose to direct law enforcement training to enhance agents' technological savvy such that policing efforts can keep pace with modern-day criminals. Further, state and local law enforcement agencies are also tasked with countering these criminal threats. As such, Congress may debate whether to provide financial, technological, or investigative support to state and local law enforcement operations.

In exercising its oversight responsibilities, Congress may examine whether law enforcement is utilizing existing mechanisms to effectively coordinate investigations and share information. US law enforcement has, particularly since the terrorist attacks of September 11, 2001, increasingly relied on intelligence-led policing, enhanced interagency cooperation (through formal and informal interagency agreements as well as fusion centers and task forces), and technological implementation to confront 21st century crime. Nonetheless, there have been notable impediments in implementing effective information sharing systems and relying on up-to-date technology. As such, policy makers may consider what is the appropriate level of interagency information sharing and whether law enforcement is effectively achieving this goal. Congress may also wish to explore whether existing inter-agency agreements are being adequately formulated, implemented, and overseen by the relevant agencies.

## End Notes

[1] For more information on the drug trafficking-related violence in Mexico, see CRS Report R41576, *Mexico's Drug Trafficking Organizations: Source and Scope of the Rising Violence*, by June S. Beittel.

[2] US Department of Justice, *FY2012 Performance Budget, Drug Enforcement Administration, US Department of Justice, Congressional Budget Submission*, p. 11, http://www.justice.gov/jmd/2012justification/pdf/fy12-deajustification.pdf.

[3] US Government Accountability Office, *Law Enforcement Coordination: DOJ Could Improve Its Process for Identifying Disagreements Among Agents*, GAO-11-314, April 2011, p. 2, http://www.gao.gov/new.items/d11314.pdf. See also US Department of Justice, Office of the Inspector General, Audit Division, *The Federal Bureau of Investigation's Ability to Address the National Security Cyber Intrusion Threat*, Audit Report 11-22, April 2011, pp. iv-vii, http://www.justice.gov/oig/reports/FBI/a1122r.pdf.

[4] See US Congress, Senate Committee on the Judiciary, Subcommittee on Crime and Terrorism, *Cybersecurity: Responding to the Threat of Cyber Crime and Terrorism*, 112th Cong., 1st sess., April 12, 2011.

[5] For more information, see archived CRS Report RL33659, *Border Security: Barriers Along the US InternationalBorder*, by Chad C. Haddal and Michael John Garcia.

[6] David R. Johnson and David Post, "Law and Borders—The Rise of Law in Cyberspace," *Stanford Law Review*, vol. 48 (May 1996), p. 1370.

[7] See the Appendix of CRS Report R41118, *Organized Retail Crime*, by Kristin M. Finklea.

[8] National Intelligence Council, *Global Trends 2025: A Transformed World*, NIC 2008-003, November 2008, p. 17,http://www.dni.gov/nic/PDF_2025/2025_Global_Trends_Final_Report.pdf.

[9] CRS Report R41237, *People Crossing Borders: An Analysis of US Border Protection Policies*, by Alison Siskin.

[10] Ibid.

[11] James C. Howell and John P. Moore, *History of Street Gangs in the United States*, US Department of Justice, Bureau of Justice Assistance, Office of Juvenile Justice and Delinquency Prevention, May 2010, http://www.ojp.usdoj.gov/BJA/pdf/NGC_History_Street_Gangs.pdf.

[12] Statement of US Attorney MacBride, United States Attorneys Office, "Twenty-Two Alleged Members of Sophisticated, Violent Fraudulent Document Ring Indicted," press release, February 24, 2011, http://www.justice.gov/ usao/vae/news/2011/02/20110224arellanonr.html.

[13] Ibid.

[14] A Trojan is a type of malware. It is a type of software that, once activated, can damage the host and provide back doors for malicious users to access the computer system. For more information on the various types of malware, see Cisco, *What Is the Difference: Viruses, Worms, Trojans, and Bots?*, http://www.cisco.com/web/about/security/ intelligence/virus-worm-diffs.html.

[15] "SpyEye vs. ZeuS Rivalry," *krebsonsecurity.com*, April 1, 2010, http://krebsonsecurity.com/2010/04/spyeye-vs-zeusrivalry/. See also Nick Farrell, "Cyber gangs fight turf war, From Russia with Love," *TechEye.net*, February 10, 2011, http://www.techeye.net/security/cyber-gangs-fight-turf-war.

[16] "SpyEye vs. ZeuS Rivalry Ends in Quiet Merger," *krebsonsecurity.com*, October 24, 2010, http://krebsonsecurity.com/2010/10/spyeye-v-zeus-rivalry-ends-in-quiet-merger/.

[17] David R. Johnson and David Post, "Law and Borders—The Rise of Law in Cyberspace," *Stanford Law Review*, vol. 48 (May 1996), p. 1379.

[18] David R. Johnson and David Post, "Law and Borders—The Rise of Law in Cyberspace," *Stanford Law Review*, vol. 48 (May 1996), p. 1370.

[19] Internet World Stats, *Internet Usage Statistics, The Internet Big Picture, World Internet Users and Population Stats*, http://www.internetworldstats.com/stats.htm.

[20] United Nations Office on Drugs and Crime, *The Globalization of Crime: A Transnational Organized Crime ThreatAssessment*, ISBN: 978-92-1-130295-0, 2010, p. 203, http://www.unodc.org/documents/data-and-analysis/tocta/TOCTA_Report_2010_low_res. pdf.

[21] The 112th Congress has held several hearings on such threats. See, for example, US Congress, House Committee onthe Judiciary, Subcommittee on Intellectual Property, Competition and the Internet, *Cybersecurity: InnovativeSolutions to Challenging Problems*, 112th Cong., 1st sess., May 25, 2011; and US Congress, House Committee on the Judiciary, Subcommittee on Crime, Terrorism, and Homeland Security, *Data Retention as a Tool for InvestigatingInternet Child Pornography and Other Internet Crimes*, 112th Cong., 1st sess., January 25, 2011.

[22] The Internet Assigned Numbers Authority (IANA) is responsible for managing internet domain names, the InternetProtocol addressing systems, and the Autonomous System Numbers used for routing internet traffic. Seehttp://www.iana.org/. See also CRS Report 97-868, *Internet Domain Names: Background and Policy Issues*, byLennard G. Kruger.

[23] Testimony by Jason Weinstein, Criminal Division, US Department of Justice, before US Congress, Senate Committee on the Judiciary, Subcommittee on Crime and Terrorism, *Cybersecurity: Responding to the Threat of Cyber Crime and Terrorism*, 112th Cong., 1st sess., April 12, 2011, http://www.justice.gov/criminal/pr/testimony/2011/crmtestimony-110412.html.

[24] Federal Bureau of Investigation, "US Indicts Ohio Man and Two Foreign Residents in Alleged Ukraine-Based 'Scareware' Fraud Scheme That Caused $100 Million in Losses to Internet Victims Worldwide," press release, May 27, 2010, http://chicago.fbi.gov/dojpressrel/pressrel10/cg052710.htm. Scareware is fake security software that appears to be legitimate. It misleads users into purchasing fake anti-virus or hard drive cleanup software

that may prove to be malicious. For more information, see Gregg Keizer, "Windows Scareware Fakes Impending Drive Disaster," *ComputerWorld*, May 16, 2011, http://www.computerworld.com/s/article/9216765/Windows_scareware_fakes_impending_drive_disaster?taxonomyId=17.

[25] For more information, see Daniel C. Richman, "The Changing Boundaries Between Federal and Local Law Enforcement," *Boundary Changes in Criminal Justice Organizations*, pp. 81-111, http://www.ncjrs.gov/ criminal_justice2000/vol_2/02d2.pdf. For a legal discussion of state sovereignty and federalism issues, see CRS Report RL30315, *Federalism, State Sovereignty, and the Constitution: Basis and Limits of Congressional Power*, by Kenneth R. Thomas.

[26] ORC typically refers to large-scale retail theft and fraud by organized groups of professional shoplifters, or "boosters." A booster is someone who steals merchandise and then sells it to a "fence" for a profit. A fence is someone who knowingly buys illegally obtained goods from a booster and then sells the goods for a profit. For more information on ORC, see CRS Report R41118, *Organized Retail Crime*, by Kristin M. Finklea.

[27] "Organized Retail Crime Jumps to 92%," *Retailer Daily*, June 10, 2009, pp. http://www.retailerdaily.com/entry/ 41799/organized-retail-crime-jumps/.

[28] US Department of Justice, "New Jersey Man Sentenced to 13 Years in Federal Prison," press release, June 17, 2010, http://www.justice.gov/usao/ncw/press/mendoza.html.

[29] Jerry Markon, "FBI-ATF Turf Battle Hurts Bomb Probes, Official Says," *The Washington Post*, August 27, 2010, http://www.washingtonpost.com/wp-dyn/content/article/2010/08/26/AR2010082606631.html. See also Jerry Markon, "FBI, ATF Battle for Control Of Cases: Cooperation Lags Despite Merger," *Washington Post*, May 10, 2008, http://www.washingtonpost.com/wp-dyn/content/article/2008/05/09/AR2008050903096.html.

[30] US Department of Justice, Office of the Inspector General, *Review of ATF's Project Gunrunner*, I-2011-001, November 2010, http://www.justice.gov/oig/reports/ATF/e1101.pdf. See also US Immigration and Customs Enforcement, "ATF, ICE update partnership agreement to maximize investigative efforts," press release, June 30, 2009, http://www.ice.gov/news/releases/0906/090630albuquerque. htm.

[31] See, for example, Joe Palazzolo, "Rival Agencies Agree to Halt Turf Battles," August 10, 2009, http://www.mainjustice.com/2009/08/10/justice-department-and-immigration-and-customs-enforcement-forge-newpartnership/.

[32] Moisés Naím, *Illicit: How Smugglers, Traffickers, and Copycats are Hijacking the Global Economy* (New York: Anchor Books, 2005), p. 13.

[33] This tunnel bust resulted in the seizure of more than two tons of marijuana. US Drug Enforcement Administration, "DEA/ICE Uncover 'Massive' Cross-Border Drug Tunnel, Cement lined passage thought to link warehouses in Tijuana and Otay Mesa," press release, January 26, 2006, http://www.justice.gov/dea/pubs/pressrel/pr012606.html.

[34] This Task Force was created in 2003 as a partnership between ICE, DEA, and the USBP, along with state law enforcement and Mexican counterparts.

[35] US Drug Enforcement Administration, "Discovery of 2nd Major San Diego-Area Cross-Border Drug Tunnel Leadsto 8 Arrests, Seizure of More Than 20 Tons of Marijuana," press release, November 26, 2010, http://www.justice.gov/dea/pubs/states/newsrel/2010/ sd112610.html.

[36] The Federal Aviation Administration (FAA) does not classify ultralights as "aircraft." For the FAA definition of anultralight, see the Code of Federal Regulations (CFR) Title 14, Section 103, http://ecfr.gpoaccess.gov/cgi/t/text/textidx?c=ecfr&sid=77f64066b8e425c01339f918e6e9f291&rgn=div5&view=text&node=14:2.0.1.3.16&idno=14.

[37] "Self-Propelled Semi-Submersible (SPSS) Watercraft," *GlobalSecurity.org*, June 28, 2008, http://www.globalsecurity.org/military/world/para/spss.htm. See also "Waving, Not Drowning: Cocaine Now Movesby Submarine," *The Economist*, May 1, 2008, http://www.economist.com/node/11294435?story_id=11294435.

[38] Rear Admiral Vincent Atkins, US Coast Guard, Testimony before the House Subcommittee on Homeland Security, on Department of Homeland Security Air and Marine Operations and

Investments, April 19, 2010, http://www.dhs.gov/ynews/testimony/testimony_1271690 315007.shtm.

[39] Drop baskets can carry over 300 pounds of marijuana or other drugs.

[40] Richard Marosi, "Ultralight Aircraft Now Ferrying Drugs Across US-Mexico Border," *Los Angeles Times*, May 19, 2011, http://www.latimes.com/news/local/la-me-border-ultralight-20110520,0,7315999.story.

[41] "Mexican Drug Cartels Use Catapult to Launch Drug Packages Across Border," *Homeland Security Newswire*, January 27, 2011, http://homelandsecuritynewswire.com/mexican-drug-cartels-use-catapult-launch-drug-packagesacross-border.

[42] "Smugglers Use Portable Ramp to Jump Border Fence," *Homeland Security Newswire*, April 19, 2011, http://homelandsecuritynewswire.com/smugglers-use-portable-ramp-jump-order-fence. See also Chris McDaniel,"Smugglers Improvise Ramp to Drive Over Border Fence," *Yuma Sun*, April 8, 2011, http://www.yumasun.com/articles/border-69033-fence-ramp.html.

[43] Federico Varese, *Mafias on the Move: How Organized Crime Conquers New Territories* (Princeton, NJ: PrincetonUniversity Press, 2011), pp. 7-8.

[44] Ibid. p. 8.

[45] For a detailed discussion of extraterritorial jurisdiction, see CRS Report 94-166, *Extraterritorial Application of American Criminal Law*, by Charles Doyle.

[46] For a list of countries with which the United States has an extradition agreement, see 18 USC. § 3181. The United States maintains diplomatic relations with a number of countries with which it does not share an extradition treaty. For instance, while the United States has diplomatic relations with China and Russia, it does not share extradition treaties with these nations.

[47] US Government Accountability Office, *Cybercrime: Public and Private Entities Face Challenges in Addressing Cyber Threats*, GAO-07-705, June 2007, p. 41, http://www.gao.gov/new.items/d07705.pdf.

[48] International Center for Missing and Exploited Children (ICMEC), *Results of the Global Child Pornography Study*, 2006, http://www. icmec.org/en_ X1/pdf/SummerNewsletter2006 formatted.pdf. ICMEC is a nonprofit organizationbased in Virginia whose goal is to protect children from sexual exploitation and abduction.

[49] US Department of Justice, "Remarks of Kevin DiGregory, Fighting Cybercrime—What are the Challenges facingEurope?," press release, September 19, 2000, http://www.justice.gov/criminal/cybercrime/EUremarks.htm.

[50] The Philippine Congress subsequently passed a law specifically dealing with computer-related crimes. WayneArnold, "Philippines to Drop Charges on E-Mail Virus," *The New York Times*, August 22, 2000, http://www.nytimes.com/2000/08/22/business/technology-philippines-to-drop-charges-on-e-mail-virus.html.

[51] For more information on federal crime control issues, see CRS Report R40812, *Federal Crime Control Issues in the111th Congress*, by Kristin M. Finklea.

[52] These include statutes such as the Racketeer Influenced and Corrupt Organizations (RICO) provisions, money laundering, and transportation or sale of stolen goods provisions.

[53] Testimony by law enforcement representatives from the FBI, ICE, USSS, and USPIS before the US Congress, House Committee on the Judiciary, Subcommittee on Crime, Terrorism, and Homeland Security, *Combating Organized Retail Crime: The Role of Federal Law Enforcement*, 111th Cong., 1st sess., November 5, 2009.

[54] For more information on COPS, see CRS Report RL33308, *Community Oriented Policing Services (COPS): Background and Funding*, by Nathan James; and CRS Report R40709, *Community Oriented Policing Services (COPS): Current Legislative Issues*, by Nathan James.

[55] For more information on JAG, see CRS Report RS22416, *Edward Byrne Memorial Justice Assistance Grant (JAG) Program*, by Nathan James.

[56] For more information on the evolution of organized crime, see CRS Report R41547, *Organized Crime: An Evolving Challenge for US Law Enforcement*, by Jerome P. Bjelopera and Kristin M. Finklea.

[57] Verizon RISK Team and US Secret Service, *2010 Data Breach Investigations Report*, p. 58.

[58] Ibid.

[59] The USSS has identified some specialized roles as carders who traffic and exploit stolen financial data, hackers and security technologists, spammers, bot herders, money launderers, internet developers and host providers, malware developers, document forgers, information service providers, hardware providers, calling services, and drop/money mule managers. Ibid., p. 59.

[60] Kimberly Kiefer Peretti, *Data Breaches: What the Underground World of "Carding" Reveals*, US Department of Justice, Computer Crime and Intellectual Property Section, p. 9, http://www.justice.gov/criminal/cybercrime/ DataBreachesArticle.pdf.

[61] US Department of Justice, "Alleged International Credit Card Trafficker Arrested in France on US Charges Related to Sale of Stolen Card Data," press release, August 11, 2010, http://www.justice.gov/opa/pr/2010/August/10crm-921.html.

[62] Michael Kenney, *From Pablo to Osama: Trafficking and Terrorist Networks, Government Bureaucracies, and Competitive Adaptation* (University Park, PA: The Pennsylvania State University Press, 2007), p. 5. Hereinafter: Kenney, *From Pablo to Osama.*

[63] For more information on intelligence sharing, see CRS Report R41848, *Intelligence Information: Need-to-Know vs. Need-to-Share*, by Richard A. Best Jr.

[64] Ibid. See also Kenney, *From Pablo to Osama*, p. 7, 103.

[65] Kenney, *From Pablo to Osama*, p. 7.

[66] The FBI partners with the National White Collar Crime Center (NW3C) to form the IC3. The IC3 serves the broad law enforcement community to receive, develop, and refer internet crime complaints.

[67] Internet Crime Complaint Center, *2010 Internet Crime Report*, p. 9, http://ic3report.nw3c.org/docs/2010_IC3_Report_02_10_11_low_res.pdf.

[68] Botnets are groups of computers that are remotely controlled by hackers. They have been infected by downloading malicious software and are used to carry out malicious activities on behalf of the hackers.

[69] *US v. John Doe*, Complaint, April 11, 2011, US District Court of Connecticut, http://newhaven.fbi.gov/dojpressrel/ pressrel11/pdf/nh041311_4.pdf.

[70] Federal Bureau of Investigation, "Department of Justice Takes Action to Disable International Botnet: More Than Two Million Computers Infected with Keylogging Software as Part of Massive Fraud Scheme," press release, April 13, 2011, http://newhaven.fbi.gov/dojpressrel/pressrel11/nh041311.htm.

[71] *US v. John Doe*, Complaint, April 11, 2011, US District Court of Connecticut, http://newhaven.fbi.gov/dojpressrel/ pressrel11/pdf/nh041311_4.pdf.

[72] Kim Zetter, "FBI vs. Coreflood Botnet: Round 1 Goes to the Feds," *Wired.com*, April 26, 2011, http://www.wired.com/threatlevel/2011/04/coreflood_results/.

[73] Federal Bureau of Investigation, "Common Fraud Schemes," http://www.fbi.gov/majcases/fraud/fraudschemes.htm. For more information on the development of AFF scams, see CRS Report R41547, *Organized Crime: An Evolving Challenge for US Law Enforcement*, by Jerome P. Bjelopera and Kristin M. Finklea.

[74] US Department of Justice, "Nigerian National Sentenced in North Carolina to 108 Months in Prison for Role in Advance Fee Fraud Scheme," press release, February 24, 2011, http://www.justice.gov/opa/pr/2011/February/11-crm242.html.

[75] See Federal Bureau of Investigation, "Gordon M. Snow, Assistant Director, Cyber Division, Federal Bureau of Investigation, Statement Before the Senate Judiciary Committee, Subcommittee on Crime and Terrorism," April 11, 2011, http://www.fbi.gov/news/testimony/cybersecurity-responding-to-the-threat-of-cyber-crime-and-terrorism. See also White House, *International Strategy for Cyberspace: Prosperity, Security, and Openness in*

*a Networked World*, May 2011, p. 4, http://www.whitehouse.gov/sites/default/files/rss_viewer/international_strategy_for_cyberspace.pdf.

[76] US Immigration and Customs Enforcement, "Chinese National Sentenced to More Than 7 Years in Federal Prison for Trafficking Counterfeit Pharmaceutical Weight-Loss Drug," press release, June 3, 2011, http://www.ice.gov/news/ releases/1106/110603denver.htm.

[77] US Immigration and Customs Enforcement, "Chinese National Sentenced to More Than 7 Years in Federal Prison for Trafficking Counterfeit Pharmaceutical Weight-Loss Drug," press release, June 3, 2011, http://www.ice.gov/news/ releases/1106/110603denver.htm.

[78] US Food and Drug Administration, "FDA Warns Consumers about Counterfeit Alli," press release, January 18, 2010, http://www.fda.gov/NewsEvents/Newsroom/PressAnnouncements/ucm197857.htm.

[79] Federal Bureau of Investigation, Steven R. Chabinsky, Deputy Assistant Director, Cyber Division at the GovSec/FOSE Conference, March 23, 2010, http://www.fbi.gov/news/speeches/the-cyber-threat-whos-doing-what-towhom.

[80] Financial Action Task Force on Money Laundering, *Report on Money Laundering Typologies: 2000 - 2001*, February 1, 2001, p. 3, http://www.fatf-gafi.org/dataoecd/29/36/34038090.pdf.

[81] Nick Wingfield, "Spam Network Shut Down," *WSJ.com*, March 18, 2011, http://online.wsj.com/article/SB10001424052748703328404576207173861008758.html?KEYWORDS=nick+wingfield.

[82] Microsoft, "Taking Down Botnets: Microsoft and the Rustock Botnet," March 17, 2011, http://blogs.technet.com/b/microsoft_on_the_issues/archive/2011/03/18/taking-down-botnets-microsoft-and-the-rustock-botnet.aspx.

[83] US Department of Justice, "Russian Man Charged with Sending Thousands of Spam Emails," press release, December 3, 2010, http://www.justice.gov/usao/wie/press_releases/2010/pr20101203_Russian_Press_release.pdf.

[84] Xinyuan Wang and Daniel Ramsbrock, "The Botnet Problem," *Computer and Information Security Handbook*, ed. John R. Vacca (Elsevier Inc., 2009), p. 129.

[85] Europol, *EU Organized Threat Assessment: OCTA 2011*, File No. 2530-274, April 28, 2011, p. 6, http://www.europol.europa.eu/publications/European_Organised_Crime_Threat_Assessment_%28OCTA%29/OCTA_2011.pdf.

[86] Legislation was introduced in the 111$^{th}$ Congress (H.R. 5127) that would have, among other things, classified stored-value cards as monetary instruments in order to require individuals to declare to Customs over $10,000 that they arecarrying on a stored value card.

[87] 31 USC. § 5312(a)(3) defines a monetary instrument as "(A) United States coins and currency; (B) as the Secretarymay prescribe by regulation, coins and currency of a foreign country, travelers' checks, bearer negotiable instruments,bearer investment securities, bearer securities, stock on which title is passed on delivery, and similar material; and (C) as the Secretary of the Treasury shall provide by regulation for purposes of sections 5316 and 5331 , checks, drafts, notes, money orders, and other similar instruments which are drawn on or by a foreign financial institution and are not in bearer form."

[88] 31 C.F.R. § 103.23(a).

[89] FinCEN, under the Department of the Treasury, administers the BSA and the nation's financial intelligence unit. FinCEN also supports law enforcement, intelligence, and regulatory agencies by analyzing and sharing financialintelligence information. For more information, see http://www.fincen.gov/about_fincen/wwd/strategic.html.

[90] US Department of the Treasury, FinCEN, "Financial Crimes Enforcement Network; Amendment to the Bank Secrecy Act Regulations—Definitions and Other Regulations Relating to Prepaid Access," 75 *Federal Register*, pp. 36589 – 36608, June 28, 2010, http://edocket.access.gpo.gov/2010/pdf/2010-15194.pdf.

[91] GAO, *Moving Illegal Proceeds: Challenges Exist in the Federal Government's Effort to Stem Cross Border Smuggling*, October 2010, pp. 48–49.

[92] Douglas Farah, "Money Laundering and Bulk Cash Smuggling: Challenges for the Merida Initiative," in *Shared Responsibility: US-Mexico Policy Options for Confronting Organized Crime*, ed. Eric L. Olson, David A. Shirk, and Andrew D. Selee (2010).

[93] See archived CRS Report 98-905, *The Encryption Debate: Intelligence Aspects*, by Keith G. Tidball and Richard A. Best Jr.

[94] Microsoft has created a tool to help law enforcement overcome some barriers posed by its data encryption tool, BitLocker. The Computer Online Forensic Evidence Extractor (COFEE) can help law enforcement capture live data on a computer. The tool ceases to work, however, if the computer is shut down. Nancy Gohring, "Microsoft Helps Law Enforcement Get Around Encryption," *PCWorld*, April 29, 2008, http://www.pcworld.com/business center/article/145318/microsoft_helps_law_enforcement_get_around_encryption.html.

[95] Federal Bureau of Investigation, "Valerie Caproni, General Counsel, Statement Before the House Judiciary Committee, Subcommittee on Crime, Terrorism, and Homeland Security," February 17, 2011, http://www.fbi.gov/news/testimony/going-dark-lawful-electronic-surveillance-in-the-face-of-new-technologies.

[96] See Freedom of Information Act (FOIA) documents provided by the FBI to the Electronic Frontier Foundation (EFF), p. 120, http://www.eff.org/files/20110207_FBI_Going_Dark_Release_Part_4.pdf. Links to the all relevant FOIA documents provided to the EFF are referenced by Jennifer Lynch, "Newly Released Documents Detail FBI's Plan to Expand Federal Surveillance Laws," *Electronic Frontier Foundation*, February 15, 2011, http://www.eff.org/deeplinks/2011/02/newly-released-documents-detail-fbi-s-plan-expand.

[97] See Freedom of Information Act (FOIA) documents provided by the FBI to the Electronic Frontier Foundation (EFF), p. 110, http://www.eff.org/files/20110207_FBI_Going_Dark_Release_Part_4.pdf.

[98] Phil Williams, "Transnational Criminal Networks," in *Networks and Netwars: The Future of Terror, Crime, and Military*, ed. John Arquilla and David Ronfeldt (RAND, 2001), p. 82.

[99] US Department of Justice, National Drug Intelligence Center, *National Drug Threat Assessment 2010,* Product No. 2010-Q0317-001, February 2010, pp. 12-13, http://www.justice.gov/ndic/pubs38/38661/38661p.pdf.

[100] Jerry H. Ratcliffe and Travis A. Taniguchi, "Is Crime Higher Around Drug Gang Street corners? Two SpatialApproaches to the Relationship Between Gang Set Spaces and Local Crime Levels," *Crime Patterns and Analysis*, vol.1, no. 1 (2008), pp. 23 - 45.

[101] Some of the violence is also directed at the Mexican government, police, and military attempting to enforce the druglaws in Mexico. For more information on the violence, see CRS Report R41576, *Mexico's Drug Trafficking Organizations: Source and Scope of the Rising Violence*, by June S. Beittel.

[102] Viridiana Ríos and David A. Shirk, *Drug Violence In Mexico, Data and Analysis Through 2010*, University of SanDiego, Trans-Border Institute, February 2011, http://justiceinmexico.files.wordpress.com/2011/02/2011-tbidrugviolence4.pdf.

[103] Targets have also included Mexican police, military, and government officials; journalists; and civilians—includingAmericans.

[104] For more information on US and Mexican efforts to combat the DTOs, see CRS Report R41349, *US-Mexican Security Cooperation: the Mérida Initiative and Beyond* , by Clare Ribando Seelke and Kristin M. Finklea.

[105] US Department of Justice, *FY2012 Performance Budget, Drug Enforcement Administration, US Department of Justice, Congressional Budget Submission*, p. 11, http://www.justice.gov/jmd/2012justification/pdf/fy12-deajustification.pdf.

[106] Kaspersky Lab presented a forecast for the 2011–2020 information technology (IT) landscape. Forecast details are discussed in "Cybercrime Outlook 2020 From Kaspersky Lab," *securelist.com*, February 11, 2011, http://www.securelist.com/en/analysis/204792165/Cybercrime_Outlook_2020_From_Kaspersky_Lab.

[107] For more information on identity theft investigations, see CRS Report R40599, *Identity Theft: Trends and Issues*, by Kristin M. Finklea. See also International Association of Chiefs of

Police (IACP) National Law Enforcement Policy Center, *Identity Theft: Concepts and Issues Paper*, March 2002, p. 2, http://www.mrsc.org/artdocmisc/identity%20theft%20 paper.pdf.

[108] US Government Accountability Office, *Law Enforcement Coordination: DOJ Could Improve Its Process for Identifying Disagreements Among Agents*, GAO-11-314, April 2011, p. 2, http://www.gao.gov/new.items/d11314.pdf.

[109] ATF, *Project Gunrunner*, http://www.atf.gov/firearms/programs/project-gunrunner/. For more information Project Gunrunner, see CRS Report R41206, *The Bureau of Alcohol, Tobacco, Firearms and Explosives (ATF): Budget and Operations for FY2011*, by William J. Krouse.

[110] US Department of Justice, Office of the Inspector General, Review of ATF's Project Gunrunner, I-2011-001, November 2010, p. iii, http://www.justice.gov/oig/reports/ATF/ e1101.pdf.

[111] Federal Bureau of Investigation, *National Cyber Investigative Joint Task Force*, http://www. fbi.gov/about-us/investigate/cyber/ncijtf.

[112] US Department of Justice, Office of the Inspector General, Audit Division, *The Federal Bureau of Investigation'sAbility to Address the National Security Cyber Intrusion Threat*, Audit Report 11-22, April 2011, pp. iv - vii, http://www.justice.gov/oig/reports/FBI/a1122r. pdf.

[113] US Government Accountability Office, *Law Enforcement Coordination: DOJ Could Improve Its Process forIdentifying Disagreements Among Agents*, GAO-11-314, April 2011, p. 8, http://www.gao.gov/new.items/d11314.pdf.

[114] Ibid., p. 10.

[115] Office of National Drug Control Strategy, National Southwest Border Counternarcotics Strategy, June 2009, p. 25.

[116] The President's Identity Theft Task Force, *Combating Identity Theft: A Strategic Plan*, April 23, 2007, p. 55, http://www.identitytheft.gov/reports/StrategicPlan.pdf.

[117] US Department of Justice, Office of the Inspector General, *Explosives Investigation Coordination Between the Federal Bureau of Investigation and the Bureau of Alcohol, Tobacco, Firearms and Explosives*, Audit Report 10-01, October 2009, see Appendix IV and Appendix VI, http://www.justice.gov/oig/reports/plus/a1001.pdf.

[118] Ibid., p. ii.

[119] Ibid., p. iii.

[120] Ibid., p. ii.

[121] GAO has subsequently noted DOJ plans to implement an information sharing system between the FBI and ATF. US Government Accountability Office, *Opportunities to Reduce Potential Duplication in Government Programs*, GAO-11-318SP, March 2011, http://www. gao.gov/ereport/GAO-11-318SP/data_center/Homeland_security— Law_enforcement/The_ Department_of_Justice_plans_actions_to_reduce_overlap_in_explosives_investigations,_bu t_ monitoring_is_needed_to_ensure_successful_implementation#_ftnref4.

[122] Agencies represented at EPIC include DEA (which leads the center), CBP, ICE, US Coast Guard, USSS, Department of Defense (DOD), Department of the Interior, FBI, ATF, US Marshals Service, Federal Aviation Administration, National Drug Intelligence Center (NDIC), Internal Revenue Service, National Geospatial-Intelligence Agency, Joint Task Force-North, Joint Interagency Task Force-South, Texas Department of Public Safety, Texas Air National Guard, and the El Paso County Sheriff's Office. For more information on EPIC, see http://www.justice.gov/ dea/programs/epic.htm.

[123] US Department of Justice, Office of the Inspector General, *Review of the Drug Enforcement Administration's El Paso Intelligence Center*, I-2010-005, June 2010, p. ii, http://www. justice.gov/oig/reports/DEA/a1005.pdf.

[124] For more information on the NGIC, see http://www.fbi.gov/about-us/investigate/vc_ majorthefts/gangs/ngic.

[125] US Department of Justice, Office of the Inspector General, *A Review of the Department's Anti-Gang Intelligence and Coordination Centers*, I-2010-001, November 2009, http://www.justice.gov/oig/reports/FBI/i2010001.pdf.

[126] Federal Bureau of Investigation, "Richard A. McFeely, Special Agent in Charge, FBI, Statement Before the Senate Judiciary Committee, Wilmington, Delaware," June 20, 2011, http://www.fbi.gov/news/testimony/information-sharingefforts-with-partners-span-many-fbi-programs.

[127] "The Advent of Netwar (Revisited)," in *Networks and Netwars: The Future of Terror, Crime, and Militancy*, ed. John Arquilla and David Ronfeldt, p. 15.

[128] Ibid., p. 18.

[129] Robert McMillan, "FBI Embeds Cyber-Investigators in Ukraine, Estonia," *PCWorld*, March 4, 2010, http://www.pcworld.com/article/190837/fbi_embeds_cyberinvestigators_in_ukraine_estonia.html. Embedding agents with international law enforcement partners allows US and foreign law enforcement to work together (in the same location) to counter specific threats.

[130] Ibid.

[131] RBS WorldPay is an Atlanta, GA-based credit card processing company that is part of the Royal Bank of Scotland. For more information on this case, see US Department of Justice, "Alleged International Hacking Ring Caught in $9 Million Fraud," press release, November 10, 2009, http://www.justice.gov/opa/pr/2009/November/09-crm-1212.html.

[132] Ibid.

[133] US Department of Justice, "International Hacker Arraigned After Extradition," press release, August 6, 2010, http://www.justice.gov/usao/gan/press/2010/08-06-10.pdf.

[134] For more information, see Drug Enforcement Administration, "Twenty Alleged Members and Associates of Colombia's Largest Drug Cartel Charged," press release, June 2, 2011, http://www.justice.gov/dea/pubs/states/newsrel/ 2011/boston060211.html.

[135] "Drug money laundering ring with ties to Colombia and Italy busted in Boston," *The Boston Globe*, June 2, 2011, http://www.boston.com/news/local/breaking_news/2011/06/multi-million_m.html.

[136] The G8 was established in 1975 as a forum for world leaders to discuss economic issues. It has since expanded to include subgroups, one of which focuses on high tech crime.

[137] United Nations Office of Drugs and Crime, *United Nations Convention Against Transnational Organized Crime and the Protocols Thereto*, United Nations, New York, 2004.

[138] From remarks by Bruce Swartz, Deputy Assistant Attorney General, Criminal Division, US Department of Justice, at US Congress, Senate Committee on Foreign Relations, *Hearing on Law Enforcement Treaties: Treaty Doc. 107-18, Inter-American Convention Against Terrorism; Treaty Doc. 108-6, Protocol of Amendment to the International Convention on the Simplification and Harmonization of Customs Procedures; Treaty Doc. 108-11, Council of Europe Convention on Cybercrime; Treaty Doc. 108-16, U.N. Convention Against Transnational Organized Crime and Protocols on Trafficking in Persons and Smuggling of Migrants*, 108th Cong., 2nd sess., June 17, 2004, pp. 29-37.

[139] For more information on the Convention, see archived CRS Report RS21208, *Cybercrime: The Council of Europe Convention*, by Kristin Archick. A copy of the Convention is available at http://conventions.coe.int/Treaty/EN/Treaties/ html/185.htm.

[140] The US Senate ratified the Convention on August 3, 2006. For the current list of signatories and ratifications, see http://conventions.coe.int/Treaty/Commun/ChercheSig.asp?NT=185&CM=1&DF=&CL=ENG.

[141] US Department of Justice, *Background on the G8*, http://www.justice.gov/criminal/cybercrime/g82004/ g8_background.html.

[142] Ibid.

[143] Statement of Janice Ayala, Deputy Assistant Director, Office of Investigations, US Immigration and Customs Enforcement, Department of Homeland Security, before the US Congress, House Committee on Homeland Security, Subcommittee on Border, Maritime,

and Global Counterterrorism, *Cargo Security at Land Ports of Entry: Are We Meeting the Challenge?*, 111th Cong., 1st sess., October 22, 2009.

[144] US Department of Justice, Office of the Inspector General, Review of ATF's Project Gunrunner, I-2011-001, November 2010, p. vi, http://www.justice.gov/oig/reports/ATF/e1101.pdf.

[145] According to DOJ, deconfliction means "ensure[ing] that two or more agencies are not duplicating resources or that one agency's investigation will not have a negative impact on another agency's investigation." In other words, deconfliction is intended, in part, to reduce turf battles. See US Department of Justice, "ICE and DOJ Sign Agreements to Share Information on Drug Trafficking and Organized Crime," press release, August 10, 2009, http://www.justice.gov/opa/pr/2009/August/09-crm-784.html.

[146] Statement of Janice Ayala, Deputy Assistant Director, Office of Investigations, US Immigration and Customs Enforcement, Department of Homeland Security, before the US Congress, House Committee on Homeland Security, Subcommittee on Border, Maritime, and Global Counterterrorism, *Cargo Security at Land Ports of Entry: Are We Meeting the Challenge?*, 111th Cong., 1st sess., October 22, 2009.

[147] US Department of Justice, "ICE and DOJ Sign Agreements to Share Information on Drug Trafficking and Organized Crime," press release, August 10, 2009, http://www.justice.gov/opa/pr/2009/August/09-crm-784.html.

[148] Department of Homeland Security, *Fusion Centers and Joint Terrorism Task Forces*, February 28, 2011, http://www.dhs.gov/files/programs/gc_1298911926746.shtm.

[149] P.L. 110-53, Aug. 3, 2007, §511, 121 STAT. 322. Amends *Homeland Security Act of 2002* by adding §210A(j).

[150] Department of Homeland Security, *Fusion Centers and Joint Terrorism Task Forces*, February 28, 2011, http://www.dhs.gov/files/programs/gc_1298911926746.shtm.

[151] There are some entities that are hybrid centers, focusing both on intelligence and operations. The National Counter Terrorism Center (NCTC), for example, is a center for joint intelligence and operational planning. Similarly, the National Intellectual Property Rights Coordination Center (IPR Center) serves as an information repository as well as a place to develop initiatives and coordinate law enforcement investigations.

[152] The FBI leads 160 Violent Gang Safe Streets Task Forces around the country. For more information, see http://www.fbi.gov/about-us/investigate/vc_majorthefts/gangs/violent-gangs-task-forces.

[153] The USSS leads 28 Electronic Fraud Task Forces. Information provided to CRS by USSS Congressional Affairs. For more information, see http://www.secretservice.gov/ectf.shtml.

[154] For more information on fusion centers, see archived CRS Report RL34070, *Fusion Centers: Issues and Options forCongress*, by John Rollins.

[155] 21 USC. § 1706.

[156] Office of National Drug Control Policy, The High-Intensity Drug Trafficking Area Program: An Overview,http://whitehousedrugpolicy.gov/hidta/overview.html.

[157] Ibid. Four main criteria are considered when designating an area as a HIDTA: "(1) the extent to which the area is a significant center of illegal drug production, manufacturing, importation, or distribution; (2) the extent to which State,local, and tribal law enforcement agencies have committed resources to respond to the drug trafficking problem in thearea, thereby indicating a determination to respond aggressively to the problem; (3) the extent to which drug-relatedactivities in the area are having a significant harmful impact in the area, and in other areas of the country; and (4) theextent to which a significant increase in allocation of Federal resources is necessary to respond adequately to drugrelated activities in the area."

[158] US Department of Justice, "Twenty-Four Defendants Federally Indicted in Southeast Wisconsin Drug Trafficking and Illegal Gambling Case," press release, June 2, 2011, http://www.justice.gov/usao/wie/press_releases/2011/pr20110602_24_Defendants_Indicted_Drug_Trafficking-Illegal_Gambling.pdf.

[159] US Department of Justice, Office of the Inspector General, *Review of the Drug Enforcement Administration's El Paso Intelligence Center*, I-2010-005, June 2010, p. ii, http://www.justice.gov/oig/reports/DEA/a1005.pdf.

[160] US Department of Justice, *FY2012 Budget and Performance Summary*, Interagency Crime and Drug Enforcement(ICDE), http://www.justice.gov/jmd/2012summary/pdf/fy12-icde-bud-summary.pdf.

[161] Data provided to CRS by USAO Congressional Affairs.

[162] Department of Homeland Security, US Immigration and Customs Enforcement (ICE), *Fact Sheet:* BorderEnforcement Security Task Forces, August 2010, http://www. ice.gov/news/library/factsheets/best.htm.

[163] For more information, see http://www.stopfraud.gov/.

[164] Federal Bureau of Investigation, "E-Bay Fraudster Sentenced to 12½ Years in Prison ," press release, May 31, 2011, http://www.fbi.gov/lasvegas/press-releases/2011/e-bay-fraudster-sentenced-to-12-1-2-years-in-prison.

[165] US Department of Justice, Office of the Inspector General, Audit Division, *The Federal Bureau of Investigation'sAbility to Address the National Security Cyber Intrusion Threat*, Audit Report 11-22, April 2011, pp. ii - iii, http://www.justice.gov/oig/reports/ FBI/a1122r.pdf. See also Federal Bureau of Investigation, *National CyberInvestigative Joint Task Force*, http://www.fbi.gov/about-us/investigate/cyber/ncijtf.

[166] See remarks of Robert S. Mueller, III, Director, Federal Bureau of Investigation, "International Conference on Cyber Security 2010," August 5, 2010, http://www.fbi.gov/news/speeches/using-partnerships-to-combat-cyber-threats.

[167] Federal Bureau of Investigation, "FBI, Slovenian and Spanish Police Arrest Mariposa Botnet Creator, Operators," press release, July 28, 2010, http://www.fbi.gov/news/pressrel/press-releases/fbi-slovenian-and-spanish-police-arrestmariposa-botnet-creator-operators.

[168] The continuum between need to know and need to share has most often been discussed in the arena of counterterrorism intelligence information sharing. See, for instance, US Congress, House Committee on Government Reform, *Moving From "Need to Know" to Need to Share": A Review of the 9/11 Commission's Recommendations*, 108th Cong., 2nd sess., August 3, 2004.

[169] Michael E. Buerger, Karen E. Gardner, and Bernard H. Levin, et al., *Incorporating Local Police Agencies Into a National Intelligence Network*, Futures Working Group, Futures Working Group White Paper Series, Vol. 1, No. 1, July 2008, pp. 42-43, http://fwg.cos.ucf.edu/publications/LocalIntel.pdf.

[170] For more information on the ISE, see CRS Report R40901, *Terrorism Information Sharing and the Nationwide Suspicious Activity Report Initiative: Background and Issues for Congress*, by Jerome P. Bjelopera. See also http://www.ise.gov/.

[171] For more databases, see the Justice Research and Statistics Association (JRSA), *Information Sharing Systems: A Survey of Law Enforcement*, July 31, 2006, p. 14, http://www.jrsa.org/pubs/reports/improving-crime-data/ Info_Sharing.pdf.

[172] Ibid, p. 6. JSRA surveyed law enforcement analysts, Statistical Analysis Center directors, and Uniform Crime Reporting program managers.

[173] Ibid., p. 7.

[174] US Department of Justice, United States Attorney, Eastern District of Pennsylvania, *Launch of the National Identity Crime Law Enforcement Network (NICLE)*, http://www.theiacp.org/investigateid/pdf/appendices/Launch-ofthe-Natitonal-Identity-Crime-Law-Enforcement-Network-NICLE.pdf.

[175] The RISS program is funded and administered by DOJ's Bureau of Justice Assistance. For more information, see http://www.riss.net/.

[176] The President's Identity Theft Task Force, *Combating Identity Theft: A Strategic Plan*, April 23, 2007, p. 56, http://www.identitytheft.gov/reports/StrategicPlan.pdf.

[177] http://www.infragard.net/index.php.

[178] Federal Bureau of Investigation, *InfraGard: A Parnership That Works*, March 8, 2010, http://www.fbi.gov/news/ stories/2010/march/infragard_030810.

[179] Statement of Steven R. Chabinsky, Deputy Assistant Director, Cyber Division, Federal Bureau of Investigation, before the US Congress, Senate Committee on the Judiciary, Subcommittee on Terrorism and Homeland Security, *Cybersecurity: Preventing Terrorist Attacks and Protecting Privacy Rights in Cyberspace*, 111th Cong., 1st sess.,November 17, 2009.

[180] Federal Bureau of Investigation, *Domestic Security: Combating Crime, Protecting Commerce*, March 14, 2011, http://www.fbi.gov/news/stories/2011/march/security_031411.

[181] For more information on LERPnet, see http://www.lerpnet2.com/.

[182] P.L. 109-162, § 1105, codified at 28 USC. § 509 note.

[183] For more information, see http://www.geophysical.com/militarysecurity.htm.

[184] Ken Stier, "Underground Threat: Tunnels Pose Trouble from Mexico to Middle East," *Time*, May 2, 2009.

[185] Office of the Director of National Intelligence, *How Do We Collect Intelligence?*, http://www.dni.gov/what_collection.htm.

[186] National Counterterrorism Center, Interagency Threat Assessment and Coordination Group, *Intelligence Guide for First Responders*, p. 7, http://www.nctc.gov/docs/itacg_guide_for_first_responders.pdf.

[187] Evan Ratliff, "The Mark; A Reporter at Large," *The New Yorker*, May 2, 2011, p. 56.

[188] Ed Pilkington, "One in four US hackers 'is an FBI informer'," *The Guardian*, June 6, 2011, http://www.guardian.co.uk/technology/2011/jun/06/us-hackers-fbi-informer.

[189] US Department of Justice, "Hacker Pleads Guilty in Manhattan Federal Court to Illegally Accessing New York Times Computer Network ," press release, January 8, 2004, http://www.justice.gov/criminal/cybercrime/lamoPlea.htm.

[190] Kevin Poulsen and Kim Zetter, "'I Can't Believe What I'm Confessing to You': The Wikileaks Chats," *Wired.com*, June 10, 2010, http://www.wired. com/threatlevel/2010/06/wikileaks-chat/.

[191] See Freedom of Information Act (FOIA) documents provided by the FBI to the Electronic Frontier Foundation (EFF), p. 120, http://www.eff.org/files/20110207_FBI_Going_Dark_Release_Part_4.pdf. Links to the all relevant FOIA documents provided to the EFF are referenced by Jennifer Lynch, "Newly Released Documents Detail FBI's Plan to Expand Federal Surveillance Laws," *Electronic Frontier Foundation*, February 15, 2011, http://www.eff.org/ deeplinks/2011/02/newly-released-documents-detail-fbi-s-plan-expand.

[192] See Freedom of Information Act (FOIA) documents provided by the FBI to the Electronic Frontier Foundation (EFF), p. 110, http://www.eff.org/files/20110207_ FBI_Going_Dark_Release_Part_4.pdf.

[193] Declan McCullagh, "FBI to Announce New Net-Wiretapping Push," *PrivacyInc*, February 16, 2011, http://news.cnet.com/8301-31921_3-20032518-281.html.

[194] Jijo Jacob, "FBI moles run illegal sites that deal in hackers' loot of sensitive data," *International Business Times*, June 7, 2011, http://www.ibtimes.com/articles/158620/20110607/fbi-hacking-hackers-hacktivists-moles-sites-lulzsecurity-lulzsec-sony-infragard-one-in-four-anonymo.htm.

In: Jurisdiction ISBN: 978-1-62081-429-1
Editors: A. Stewart and D. Washington 

*Chapter 3*

# INDIAN TRIBAL CIVIL JURISDICTION'S REACH OVER NON-INDIANS: PLAINS COMMERCE BANK V. LONG FAMILY LAND AND CATTLE CO., INC.*

***Yule Kim***

## SUMMARY

Many Indian tribes have tribal court systems where tribal laws and regulations may be enforced against tribal members. However, absent express congressional authorization, a tribal court may subject nonmembers to its civil jurisdiction for claims arising from non-Indian fee lands located within Indian reservations only if (1) the nonmember has entered into a consensual commercial relationship with the tribe or a tribal member, or (2) the conduct of the nonmember has some direct effect on the political integrity, economic security, or the health or welfare of the tribe. The Supreme Court addressed the reach of tribal civil jurisdiction over nonmembers in *Plains Commerce Bank v. Long Family Land and Cattle Co., Inc.*, 554 US ___, 128 S. Ct. 2709 (2008), a case that presents the question of whether Indian tribal courts have jurisdiction over a nonmember involved in a civil tort claim arising out of a consensual business relationship with a tribal member. In this case, tribal members had alleged that an off-reservation bank had discriminated

* This is an edited, reformatted and augmented version of a Congressional Research Service publication, CRS Report for Congress RS22820, from www.crs.gov, dated April 9, 2010.

against them by refusing to sell back land that the tribal members had previously owned and sold to the bank pursuant to a mortgage agreement. In tribal court, the tribal members brought an array of tribal common law claims, and won most of them, including the discrimination claim. The Supreme Court, however, reversed, holding that tribes cannot regulate or adjudicate claims relating to the sale of non-Indian fee lands.

## BACKGROUND

Indian tribes, prior to the signing of the US Constitution, were sovereign entities.[1] To this day, tribes largely retain their inherent sovereignty over their internal affairs.[2] However, tribal sovereignty has been viewed by the federal courts as limited, in view of the tribes' status as domestic dependent nations,[3] and is subject to the near plenary power of Congress.[4]

One aspect of inherent tribal sovereignty that remains largely intact is the power to regulate the internal affairs of the tribe that occur within the boundaries of the reservation and, in some limited situations, matters that directly affect tribal members outside of the reservation.[5] A tribe's civil jurisdiction over its members is a product of this inherent sovereignty. However, even though the federal government does not delegate jurisdiction to tribes through statutes or treaties, federal judicial decisions do impose some restrictions on the scope of tribal jurisdiction. In addition, Congress may also choose to expand or contract tribal jurisdiction through legislation.[6]

In the absence of federal legislation, federal court decisions define the parameters of tribal jurisdiction. The basic framework for tribal civil jurisdiction was established in *Montana v. United States*, which held that Indian tribes could not regulate the activities of nonmembers who are on non-Indian fee lands[7] located within Indian reservations.[8] *Montana's* original holding only addressed a tribe's civil regulatory authority over nonmembers, but has since been interpreted to limit a tribe's civil adjudicatory authority as well.[9] However, the Court in *Montana* also carved two exceptions to this restriction: tribes may assert civil jurisdiction over nonmembers on non-Indian fee lands when (1) the nonmember has entered into a consensual relationship with the tribe or its members or (2) the nonmember's conduct threatens or has some direct effect on the political integrity, the economic security, or the health or welfare of the tribe.[10]

Any attempt to determine a valid exercise of tribal civil jurisdiction begins with an analysis under *Montana*,[11] although various factors affect the precise scope of the exceptions. For example, a mere showing of a consensual relationship between a nonmember and either the tribe or a tribal member is not sufficient to support tribal civil jurisdiction.[12] The tribal exercise of authority must "take the form of taxation, licensing, or 'other means' of regulating the activities of the nonmember" and "must have some nexus to the consensual relationship."[13] In order for there to be a possibility of tribal civil jurisdiction, the lawsuit must arise from the consensual relationship itself.[14]

Although the reach of tribal court jurisdiction does not necessarily turn on the ownership status of the land upon which the dispute occurred, in most circumstances, nonmember ownership of the land is presumptively conclusive of the absence of tribal civil jurisdiction.[15]

## PLAINS COMMERCE BANK V. LONG FAMILY LAND AND CATTLE CO., INC.

### Facts of the Case

The Long Company was an Indian-owned farming and ranching business incorporated under the laws of South Dakota and located within the Cheyenne River Sioux Indian Reservation. The Company had mortgaged its land to Plains Commerce Bank, a South Dakota corporation located outside of the reservation.

The Company and the Bank later entered into a loan agreement, which provided that the Company would deed the mortgaged land to the Bank while the Bank would cancel the Company's prior debt and issue additional loans for use in the Company's ranching operations. The Company was then given a two-year lease on the property with an option to purchase. The loan agreement was negotiated within the tribe's offices under the supervision of tribal and Bureau of Indian Affairs (BIA) officers, but signed in the bank's offices off-reservation.

According to the Long family, who owned the Company, Plains Commerce Bank had initially offered more favorable purchase terms during the negotiations of the lease agreement, but later withdrew the offer, citing "possible jurisdictional problems" posed by the Long Company's status as an "Indian owned entity on the reservation." Furthermore, the Longs claimed that the bank never provided the promised operating loans and, as a result, the Long Company could not support its ranching operation through the winter of

1996-1997. Because of the loss of hundreds of livestock during that winter, the Longs lacked sufficient funds to exercise their option to repurchase the land. When the Longs did not vacate the property, Plains Commerce Bank initiated state eviction proceedings and asked the Cheyenne River Sioux Tribal Court to serve the Longs a notice to quit. Plains Commerce Bank also divided the land into separate parcels and sold these parcels to several nonmembers.

## Procedural Background

The Longs filed a complaint in tribal court alleging an array of claims, including a discrimination claim. Plains Commerce Bank answered that the tribal court lacked jurisdiction and stated a counterclaim. The tribal court found that it had jurisdiction, denied the Bank's motion for summary judgment on its counterclaim, and then proceeded to judgment. At the conclusion of the tribal court trial, the jury was instructed on four of the Longs' claims: breach of contract, bad faith, discrimination, and improper use of self-help.

A unanimous jury found for the Longs on all counts except the self-help claim, and returned a general verdict in their favor for $750,000 in damages plus interest. A later supplemental judgment further awarded the Longs an option to purchase land they still occupied, which would have nullified the Bank's previous sale of land to nonmembers.

The Bank appealed the judgment to the tribal court of appeals, arguing that tribal courts did not have jurisdiction to adjudicate violations of federal discrimination laws. The tribal appellate court held that the discrimination claim filed by the Longs arose not from federal law, but from tribal common law. Furthermore, the tribal appellate court held that the tribal court could exercise jurisdiction over the discrimination claim because the Bank had a consensual relationship with a tribal member that implicated the tribe's economic security.

Plains Commerce Bank then filed an action in federal district court seeking a declaration that the tribal judgment was not entitled to recognition because the tribal court lacked jurisdiction over the Longs' discrimination claim.[16]

The district court found that the tribal court did have jurisdiction over Plains Commerce Bank based on its consensual relationship with the Longs and their company, the clear nexus between the discrimination claim and the consensual relationship, and because tort claims, in general, fall under the rubric of the "consensual relationship" exception.

## Eighth Circuit

The Bank then appealed the district court judgment to the US Court of Appeals for the Eighth Circuit. The Eighth Circuit focused on whether there was a sufficient consensual relationship between Plains Commerce Bank and the Long Company, and then whether the suit arose from that consensual relationship.[17] The Eighth Circuit concluded that the commercial dealings between Plains Commerce Bank and the Long Company constituted a consensual relationship and that the tribe's common law discrimination cause of action was a valid means of regulating commercial dealings.[18] Therefore, the court concluded that the tribe had inherent authority to regulate a nonmember's conduct arising out of a consensual relationship through the adjudication of a tortious discrimination claim.

## US Supreme Court

Plains Commerce Bank petitioned the US Supreme Court for a writ of *certiorari* to review the Eighth Circuit decision.[19] The Supreme Court granted the petition on January 4, 2008.[20] On June 25, 2008, the Supreme Court reversed the decision of the Eighth Circuit.[21] The Court began by citing the proposition that tribal sovereignty lies upon tribal trust land and on tribal members within the reservation. But, the Court noted, tribes generally do not have such authority over non-Indians who come within the tribal borders. "This general rule thus restricts tribal authority over non-member activities taking place on the reservation, and is particularly strong when the nonmember's activity occurs on land owned in fee simple by non-Indians."[22] This is true even if the land was at one time tribal; once converted into fee simple, the tribe loses plenary authority over it. Therefore, the tribe loses the authority not only to enjoin the land's sale, but also the authority to regulate the use of fee land by way of tribal ordinance or actions in the tribal courts. The only two exceptions to this rule are the ones outlined in *Montana*.[23] The Court concluded, however, that the *Montana* exceptions apply only to the tribal authority to regulate activities conducted on non-Indian fee lands, and that *Montana* categorically does not permit tribes to regulate the sale of non-Indian fee lands.

In reciting the history of tribal civil jurisdiction, the Court noted that tribal civil jurisdiction was recognized in circumstances that involved taxation, licensing for hunting and fishing, and the sale of merchandise by a non-Indian to an Indian on the reservation.[24] The Court emphasized that the only time it had previously recognized tribal authority to regulate nonmember activity on non-Indian fee land was when it permitted restraints on land use imposed by tribal zoning regulations. Even then, the Court noted, the regulation was permitted only because of the fee land was isolated in "the heart of a closed portion of the reservation."[25]

Noting this history, the Court concluded that because tribes held limited sovereign interests, the *Montana* exceptions were meant only to permit tribal oversight of nonmember conduct that would threaten or intrude on the tribe's internal affairs or self-rule.[26]

The Court found that this proposition precludes the tribe from regulating the sale of non-Indian fee lands because the effect land ownership has on a tribe's internal affairs and self-rule ends when the land passes from tribal ownership to fee simple status. Although nonmember conduct on the land may injure the tribe's internal affairs and self-rule, this injury may only be remedied by regulating the nonmember conduct, and not by enjoining the sale of such lands to other nonmembers.[27]

In applying this reasoning to the Longs' discrimination suit, the Court characterized the suit as a means for the tribe to regulate a "non-Indian's sale of non-Indian fee land." Because the discrimination suit would have nullified such a sale, which *Montana* prohibits a tribe from doing, the Court reversed the Eighth Circuit decision.[28]

## CONCLUDING OBSERVATIONS

The *Plains Commerce Bank* case has clarified one crucial point: tribal governments may not regulate the sale of non-Indian fee lands located within the reservation. This appears to be a per se rule because the Supreme Court in its analysis concluded that such sales categorically do not implicate the legitimate tribal interests that *Montana* exceptions are meant to protect.

On the other hand, the Supreme Court has left open the possibility that the conduct of nonmembers on non-Indian fee lands can still be regulated. A remaining issue is the precise scope of tribal authority over nonmembers.

The Court may have to address in the future whether tribal jurisdiction over nonmember conduct is restricted to taxation or licensing, or if a tribe's civil jurisdiction can also encompass more extensive oversight via common law adjudications.

## End Notes

[1] Felix S. Cohen. Handbook of Federal Indian Law 205 (Nell Jessup Newton ed. 2005) [hereinafter "Cohen"]. *See also Worcester v. Georgia*, 31 US 515, 559 (1832) (characterizing Indian tribes as "distinct, independent political communities").

[2] *See* United States v. Wheeler, 435 US 313 (1978).

[3] *See* Cherokee Nation v. Georgia, 30 US 1 (1831); Worcester v. Georgia, 31 US 515 (1832).

[4] For an analysis of retained tribal sovereignty, *see* Duro v. Reina, 495 US 676 (1990); Montana v. United States, 450 US 544 (1981).

[5] Cohen, *supra* 212-219.

[6] *Id. See also* United States v. Lara, 541 US 193 (2004); 25 USC. §1301(2) (conferring on tribal courts criminal jurisdiction over Indians who are not members of the tribe).

[7] "Non-Indian fee land" refers to land that was once previously held by the federal government in trust for the benefit of an Indian tribe, but is now owned by an individual in fee simple. The federal government in 1908 had allotted several million acres of tribal trust land to individual tribal members in fee simple parcels, freeing those lands from the trust's alienability restrictions.

[8] 450 US 544 (1981).

[9] Strate v. A-1 Contractors, 520 US 438, 453 (1997) ("As to nonmembers, we hold, a tribe's adjudicative jurisdiction does not exceed its legislative jurisdiction. Absent congressional direction enlarging tribal court jurisdiction, we adhere to that understanding.").

[10] *Montana*, 450 US at 565-66.

[11] See L. Scott Gould, *The Consent Paradigm: Tribal Sovereignty At The Millennium*, 96 Colum. L. Rev. 809, 872 (1996).

[12] *Strate*, 520 US at 457 (determining that even though the nonmember was engaged in subcontract work with the tribe and was, thus, in a consensual relationship with the tribe, the tribal member suing the nonmember was not a party to the subcontract, and, thus, the lawsuit did not qualify for the consensual relationship exception to the general prohibition of tribal civil jurisdiction over nonmembers).

[13] Atkinson Trading Co. v. Shirley, 532 US 645, 656 (2001) (holding that a tribal hotel-occupancy tax was invalid when imposed on a nonmember owned hotel located on non-Indian fee land because the tax was not authorized by Congress by either treaty or statute, and it had not been established that the tax was related to a consensual relationship between the tribe and the nonmember-owned hotel or that the tax would affect the political integrity of the tribe).

[14] *Id.* ("A nonmember's consensual relationship in one area thus does not trigger tribal civil authority in another ... ").

[15] Nevada v. Hicks (*Hicks*), 533 US 353, 359-360 (2001).

[16] Plains Commerce Bank v. Long Family Land & Cattle Co., Inc., 440 F. Supp. 2d 1070 (D.S.D. 2006).

[17] Plains Commerce Bank v. Long Family Land & Cattle Co., Inc., 491 F.3d 878 (8th Cir. 2007).

[18] *Id.* at 887.

[19] 128 S. Ct. 829 (2008).

[20] *Id.*

[21] Plains Commerce Bank v. Long Family Land & Cattle Co., 554 US __ , 128 S. Ct. 2709 (2008).

[22] *Id.* at 2719.

[23] *Id.* at 2719-2720.
[24] *Id.* at 2721-2722.
[25] *Id.* at 2722.
[26] *Id.* at 2623.
[27] *Id.* at 2723-2724.
[28] *Id.* at 24.

In: Jurisdiction
Editors: A. Stewart and D. Washington ISBN: 978-1-62081-429-1


*Chapter 4*

# SUPREME COURT APPELLATE JURISDICTION OVER MILITARY COURT CASES*

*R. Chuck Mason*

## SUMMARY

Military courts, authorized by Article I of the US Constitution, have jurisdiction over cases involving military servicemembers, including, in some cases, retired servicemembers. They have the power to convict for crimes defined in the Uniform Code of Military Justice (UCMJ), including both uniquely military offenses and crimes with equivalent definitions in civilian laws. For example, in *United States v. Stevenson*, military courts prosecuted a retired serviceman for rape, a crime often tried in civilian courts.

The military court system includes military courts-martial; a Criminal Court of Appeals for each branch of the armed services; and the US Court of Appeals for the Armed Forces (CAAF), which has discretionary appellate jurisdiction over all military cases. With the exception of potential final review by the US Supreme Court, these Article I courts handle review of military cases in an appellate system that rarely interacts with Article III courts.

* This is an edited, reformatted and augmented version of Congressional Research Service, Publication No. RL34697, dated March 30, 2011.

Criminal defendants in the Article III judicial system have an automatic right to appeal to federal courts of appeal and then a right to petition the Supreme Court for final review. In contrast, defendants in military cases typically may not appeal their cases to the US Supreme Court unless the highest military court, the CAAF, had also granted discretionary review in the case.

Companion bills introduced in the 111th Congress, the Equal Justice for Our Military Act of 2010 (H.R. 569) and the Equal Justice for United States Military Personnel Act of 2009 (S. 357), would have authorized appeals to the US Supreme Court for all military cases, including cases that the CAAF declined to review. While neither of the companion bills passed their respective chamber, the House passed a similar measure, H.R. 3174, during the 110th Congress. To date, however, similar legislation has not been introduced in the 112th Congress.

## INTRODUCTION

The US military justice system exercises jurisdiction over criminal cases pursuant to Article I of the US Constitution and the Uniform Code of Military Justice (UCMJ).

Military courts' jurisdiction is limited to trying people connected to the armed forces for crimes defined by the UCMJ. Within these constraints, military courts' jurisdiction is relatively broad. For example, it extends to retired servicemembers such as the defendant in *United States v. Stevenson*,[1] a case in which military courts convicted a man on the Navy's temporary disability retired list. In *Stevenson*, the Navy prosecuted the defendant for rape, a crime routinely tried in non-military courts with civilian defendants.[2]

In general, the military justice system, including its system of appellate review, is separate and distinct from the civilian judicial system. Some constitutional safeguards and Supreme Court interpretations are inapplicable in military courts. Also, after following appellate review through the military court system, military defendants may appeal to the US Supreme Court only in limited circumstances.

Companion bills introduced in the 111th Congress, H.R. 569 and S. 357, would have broadend the Supreme Court's statutory jurisdiction by authorizing Supreme Court review of most military cases. This report surveys military courts' jurisdiction, the structure of appellate review for military cases, interactions between military and civilian courts, the *Stevenson* case, and past legislative proposals.

## MILITARY COURTS' JURISDICTION

Most criminal cases in the United States are tried either in state courts or in civilian federal courts. The latter derive authority from Article III of the US Constitution.[3] However, the armed forces may prosecute defendants with military connections in military courts, which derive authority from Article I, sec. 8 of the Constitution.[4]

The UCMJ, passed by Congress and implemented by the President through the Manual for Courts-Martial (MCM), governs military courts' jurisdiction and procedures.[5] Military courts exercise jurisdiction over officers and enlisted servicemembers on active duty.[6] However, the scope of their jurisdiction may extend beyond individuals serving on active duty. Specifically, such jurisdiction extends to cases involving retired servicemembers who receive military pay or hospital care from an armed force; specified members of reserve units; enemy combatants; and other individuals with connections to military operations or benefits.[7] As noted below in the discussion of *United States v. Stevenson*, questions remain regarding the scope of military courts' power over retired servicemembers. However, it is clear that military courts' jurisdiction extends to military veterans only when a veteran maintains at least some current relationship with the military.[8]

If a defendant's connection with the armed forces is sufficient to establish jurisdiction, a military court may try that defendant for a broad range of offenses, including conduct not related to official military duties, as long as the alleged conduct constitutes a crime under the UCMJ. The UCMJ includes some crimes that are unique to military service. For example, under the UCMJ, a defendant might be prosecuted for effecting unlawful enlistment, appointment, or separation; desertion; or absence without leave.[9] However, the armed forces may also prosecute defendants under the UCMJ for conduct over which civilian courts could also exert jurisdiction. For example, the UCMJ criminalizes murder, rape, robbery, and other common law crimes.[10]

## APPELLATE STRUCTURE FOR MILITARY CASES

Article I military courts handle military cases throughout the chain of appellate review. Appeal to the US Supreme Court is permitted at the end of the process only in specified circumstances.

The UCMJ creates various military courts and provides appellate procedures for them.[11] After an initial investigation and a court-martial, which is a trial-level proceeding, military cases undergo various stages of review within the military justice system. First, each court-martial proceeding has a "convening authority," who is a commissioned officer (other than the defendant's accuser) who convenes the investigation and court-martial proceeding and then approves or modifies the court-martial's findings and sentences.[12] Convening authorities do not provide legal review; instead, they provide the equivalent of sentencing determinations by giving "full and fair consideration to matters submitted by the accused and determining appropriate action on the sentence."[13] Under the UCMJ, convening authorities have "substantial discretion" to modify sentences and findings.[14]

After a convening authority approves or modifies a court-martial decision, a Court of Criminal Appeals offers the first opportunity for legal review in military cases. Each branch of the armed services has a Court of Criminal Appeals, comprised of panels of military judges[15] established by the Judge Advocate General for each branch.[16] The Courts of Criminal Appeals review cases in panels or, occasionally, *en banc*.[17] Review is not discretionary; each Judge Advocate General "shall refer" to the relevant Court of Criminal Appeals every case involving a conviction that imposes the death penalty or confinement for one year or more; a bad-conduct or dishonorable discharge; or, in certain cases, dismissal from the respective service.[18] Unlike convening authorities, Courts of Criminal Appeals provide legal review of military cases. They "may affirm only such findings of guilty, and the sentence ... as [they] fin[d] correct in law and fact and determin[e], on the basis of the entire record, should be approved."[19]

After a Court of Criminal Appeals has reviewed a case, the United States Court of Appeals for the Armed Forces (CAAF) provides the final opportunity for appellate review within the military court system. The CAAF is an Article I court, housed within the Department of Defense.[20] However, unlike other military courts, the CAAF is comprised of civilian judges, whom the President appoints.[21]

In general, the CAAF has discretion to grant or deny petitions for appeals, analogous to the US Supreme Court's discretion to grant or deny writs of certiorari.[22] However, the CAAF must accept appeals in two circumstances: (1) all cases in which the relevant Court of Criminal Appeals has affirmed a death sentence; and (2) all cases in which a Judge Advocate General has sent a case to the CAAF for review after a final Court of Criminal Appeals decision.[23]

The CAAF's appellate review is limited. The CAAF must act "only with respect to the findings and sentence as approved by the [court-martial's] convening authority and as affirmed or set aside as incorrect in law by the Court of Criminal Appeals."[24] In other words, appeals to the CAAF must involve issues originally heard by a court-martial and affirmed or denied by a convening authority and the relevant Court of Criminal Appeals. The CAAF cannot hear appeals based on the All Writs Act or other jurisdictional authority unless they aid direct review of court-martial decisions.

For example, in *Clinton v. Goldsmith*,[25] the Air Force had dropped from its rolls a servicemember who had served an earlier sentence for engaging in unprotected sex without telling his partners of his HIV-positive status. The servicemember had petitioned the Air Force Court of Criminal Appeals for injunctive relief under the All Writs Act, but that court denied relief, holding that it lacked jurisdiction. The CAAF then granted injunctive relief enjoining the President and other officials from dropping the servicemember from the active duty rolls.[26] The US Supreme Court held that the CAAF had exceeded its jurisdiction in granting injunctive relief because the relief did not involve review of a court-martial decision.[27] In so holding, the Supreme Court rejected the CAAF's argument that jurisdiction was proper because the Air Force's dropping of the servicemember related to conduct at issue in an earlier court-martial proceeding; instead, the Court emphasized that "there is no source of continuing jurisdiction for the CAAF over all actions administering sentences that the CAAF at one time had the power to review."[28]

With respect to appeals from the CAAF, the US Supreme Court has jurisdiction to grant certiorari in four specific circumstances: (1) cases in which a death sentence has been affirmed by the relevant branch's Court of Criminal Appeals; (2) cases that a Judge Advocate General has certified to the CAAF; (3) cases in which the CAAF granted a petition for review; and (4) cases that do not fall in the other categories but in which the CAAF has granted relief.[29] The first two categories represent the two circumstances in which the CAAF must grant appeals. The second category represents cases in which the CAAF has exercised its discretion to grant an appeal. And the final category is a catch-all provision for other cases in which the CAAF might grant relief.

Because the Supreme Court's jurisdiction is limited to these four circumstances, its power to review military cases generally extends only to cases that the CAAF has also reviewed. For this reason, the CAAF's discretion over the acceptance or denial of appeals often functions as a gatekeeper for military appellants' access to Supreme Court review. If the CAAF denies an appeal, the US Supreme Court will typically lack the authority to review the decision. In contrast, criminal appellants in Article III courts have an automatic right of appeal to federal courts of appeals and then a right to petition the Supreme Court for review.[30]

## INTERACTIONS BETWEEN ARTICLE I AND ARTICLE III COURTS

The US armed forces have a long history of self-regulation. Except for limited interaction with the US Supreme Court, Article I military courts operate separately from the Article III judicial system.

As discussed above, military courts have distinct trial procedures and structures for appellate review. In addition, because military courts' jurisdictional authority arises under Article I rather than Article III, defendants in military cases do not have the benefit of certain Article III safeguards, such as lifetime appointments for judges.[31] In addition, although military defendants are entitled to due process rights under the Fifth Amendment to the Constitution, the Supreme Court has upheld a narrowed interpretation of such rights in the context of military courts.[32]

Furthermore, legal interpretations by Article III courts do not necessarily create binding precedent for Article I courts, and vice versa. The only Article III court holdings that bind military courts are those of the US Supreme Court. However, military courts sometimes reject even Supreme Court precedents as inapplicable in the military context. For example, in *United States v. Marcum*,[33] the CAAF declined to follow an interpretation of the constitutional right to privacy that the Supreme Court had handed down a short while earlier. In *Marcum*, a court-martial had convicted a servicemember of various crimes, including non-forcible sodomy.[34]

On appeal, the servicemember argued that with respect to the non-forcible sodomy charge, he was protected by a constitutional right to privacy in intimate relations under the Supreme Court case *Lawrence v. Texas*.[35] However, the CAAF declined to follow *Lawrence*.[36] The CAAF's rationale for diverging from Supreme Court precedent in *Marcum* was that constitutional protections "may apply differently to members of the armed forces than they do to civilians."[37] Thus, although "constitutional rights identified by the Supreme Court generally apply to members of the military," such rights do not apply when "by text or scope they are plainly inapplicable."[38]

Similarly, Article III courts are not bound by military courts' decisions. The Supreme Court may consider CAAF decisions or UCMJ provisions as potentially persuasive. For example, the Supreme Court ordered briefs to examine the impact of a military code provision after it handed down its decision in *Kennedy v. Louisiana*,[39] a case involving the question of a death penalty sentence for a child rapist.[40] In *Kennedy*, the Supreme Court held that the Eighth Amendment prohibits punishment by death penalty for a defendant who rapes a child but did not cause or intend to cause a child's death.[41] In so holding, the Court emphasized the "national consensus" against the death penalty in such cases.[42] In its petition for rehearing, Louisiana argued that Congress's recent amendment of the UCMJ to include a death penalty punishment in military cases for the rape of a child undermined the Court's "national consensus" argument.[43] However, the Supreme Court decided not to reconsider its *Kennedy* decision, instead reaffirming its prior ruling with only minor modifications. In its opinion accompanying its denial of rehearing, the Supreme Court disagreed with Louisiana's interpretation of the death penalty language in the UCMJ amendment, but it also emphasized that "authorization of the death penalty in the military sphere does not indicate that the penalty is constitutional in the civilian context."[44]

## UNITED STATES V. STEVENSON

United States v. Stevenson[45] highlights two issues relevant to jurisdiction in military cases. First, it raises questions regarding the scope of military courts' jurisdiction over retired servicemembers. Second, it raises a question regarding Supreme Court jurisdiction to review legal questions when the CAAF denied review. The first question was the basis for the Stevenson appellant's petition to the Supreme Court for certiorari.[46] The United States raised the second question in its brief opposing appellant's certiorari petition.[47]

Although the US Supreme Court clearly has jurisdiction over cases in which the CAAF granted review,[48] it is unclear whether the Supreme Court's jurisdiction extends to specific issues that the CAAF declined to address. In Stevenson, Naval Criminal Investigative Service officials had investigated the appellant, a man on the Navy's temporary disability retired list, while he received treatment at a Veterans Affairs hospital. A military court-martial then tried and convicted the appellant for rape. On appeal, the CAAF remanded the case for fact finding regarding blood draws taken while appellee was a patient at the VA hospital.[49]

After the United States Navy-Marine Corps Court of Criminal Appeals affirmed the courtmartial's decision on remand, the CAAF granted a second review of the case.[50] However, exercising its discretion, the CAAF limited the issues on appeal to potential Fourth Amendment violations, declining to review the question of the military court's jurisdiction over a man on the temporary disability retired list.[51]

In his petition to the Supreme Court for certiorari, the appellant in Stevenson requested review of only the issue that the CAAF had declined to address—namely, the issue of military courts' jurisdiction over a case involving a person on the temporary disability retired list.[52] In response, the United States argued in its opposing brief that the Supreme Court's appellate review power does not extend to issues that the CAAF declined to review.[53] Thus, because the CAAF had declined to review that portion of the Criminal Court of Appeals' decision, the United States argued that the Supreme Court lacked jurisdiction over the appeal.[54] Ultimately, the Supreme Court declined to hear the case.[55]

On remand to the Navy-Marine Corps Court of Criminal Appeals, for the second time, the court set aside both the findings and the sentence and authorized a rehearing. The questions raised by the petition to the Supreme Court for certiorari remain unanswered.

## LEGISLATIVE PROPOSALS TO EXPAND JURISDICTION

Bills introduced during the 111th Congress, the Equal Justice for Our Military Act of 2010 (H.R. 569) and the Equal Justice for United States Military Personnel Act of 2009 (S. 357), would have expanded the US Supreme Court's appellate jurisdiction over military cases.[56] Specifically, the legislation would have amended the UCMJ to authorize appeals to the Supreme Court in military cases, regardless of the CAAF's acceptance or denial of an appeal.[57] Bill sponsors emphasized the need for the law to address the "disparity" between the broad right to appeal to the Supreme Court in civilian cases, on one hand, and the limited ability to appeal to the Supreme Court in military cases, on the other hand.[58] When introducing S. 357, Senator Feinstein stated that because "our US service personnel place their lives on the line in defense of American rights[, it] is unacceptable for us to continue to routinely deprive our men and women in uniform one of those rights."[59]

H.R. 569, reported to the House on July 15, 2010, as amended, included language not found in the companion bill, S. 357.[60] The amended bill authorized the Supreme Court, through its rules, to prescribe the time limit for application for a writ of certiorari of a decision of the CAAF, or the refusal of the CAAF to grant a petition of review.[61] The bill would have been effective at the conclusion of the 180-day period beginning on the date of enactment and then only to decisions of the CAAF handed down on or after that date.[62] Additionally, the bill provided that the authority of the Supreme Court to prescribe necessary rules shall take effect on the date of enactment of the act.[63] To date, similar legislation has not been introduced in the 112th Congress.

## CONCLUSION

Courts have recognized compelling justifications for a military justice system that is distinct from Article III courts. For example, in *Marcum*, the CAAF emphasized the importance of ensuring discipline and obedience in the armed forces.[64] The *Marcum* court also stressed the military's interest in disciplining servicemembers differently according to their rank.[65] However, it is unclear whether such arguments justify a disparity in access to Supreme Court review, especially in the context of servicemembers no longer on active duty or crimes that exist under both military and civilian laws.

Military cases follow a unique process of appellate review, moving from courts-martial through the following steps: (1) automatic appeals to Courts of Criminal Appeals for each armed forces branch; (2) potential discretionary review by the highest military court, the CAAF; and (3) review by the US Supreme Court in limited circumstances, usually only when the CAAF has also granted review. Legislative proposals in the 111th Congress would expand Supreme Court jurisdiction over military cases by authorizing review even if the CAAF denies an appeal. If the proposals became law, they would make moot the question highlighted by *United States v. Stevenson* regarding the Supreme Court's jurisdiction over specific issues that the CAAF had declined to review.

## End Notes

[1] 52 M.J. 504 (N-M. Ct. Crim. App. 1999), *rev'd*, 53 M.J. (C.A.A.F. 2000), *cert. denied*, 532 US 919 (2001), *remanded to* 65 M.J. 639 (N-M. Ct. Crim. App. 2006), *vacated*, 66 M.J. 15 (C.A.A.F. 2008), *cert. denied*, 129 S. Ct. 69 (2008), *vacated*, 2009 WL 4691176 (N-M. Ct. Crim. App. 2009).

[2] *Id.* at 16. In *Stevenson*, the Naval Criminal Investigative Service investigated the defendant after determining that he "was a possible suspect in a ... rape of a military dependent." *Id.* Thus, military prosecutors tried the case in military courts. However, a civilian court would have had jurisdiction over the same conduct in a case involving a civilian defendant.

[3] Article III vests judicial power in the Supreme Court and "such inferior courts as the Congress may from time to time ordain and establish." US Const. art. III. Article III courts include the US Supreme Court, federal courts of appeals, federal district courts, and the US Court of International Trade.

[4] Relevant provisions of Art. I, sec. 8 empower Congress to "raise and support armies"; "provide and maintain a navy"; and "make rules for the government and regulation of the land and naval forces." The section also grants Congress powers of "organizing, arming, and disciplining the Militia, and for governing such Part of them as may be employed in the Service of the United States." US Const. art. I, § 8.

[5] 10 USC. § 801 *et. seq.*

[6] 10 USC. § 802.

[7] 10 USC. § 802(a).

[8] Toth v. Quarles, 350 US 11, 14-15 (1955) ("It has never been intimated by this Court ... that Article I military jurisdiction could be extended to civilian ex-soldiers who had severed all relationship with the military and its institutions.").

[9] 10 USC. §§ 884, 885, 886.

[10] *Id.* at §§ 918, 920, 922.

[11] 10 USC. § 801 *et. seq.*

[12] 10 USC. § 860; United States v. Davis, 58 M.J. 100 (C.A.A.F. 2003).

[13] *Davis*, 58 M.J. at 102.

[14] 10 USC. § 860(c).

[15] The UCMJ defines "military judge" as a "commissioned officer of the armed forces" whom the Judge Advocate General of the relevant branch has certified as qualified to serve in the branch in which the judge is a member. 10 USC. § 826(b).

[16] 10 USC. § 866(a). The four Courts of Criminal Appeals are the Army Court of Criminal Appeals, the Air Force Court of Criminal Appeals, the Navy-Marine Corps' Court of Criminal Appeals, and the Coast Guard Court of Criminal Appeals.

[17] *Id.*

[18] 10 USC. § 866(b). Dismissals of commissioned officers, cadets, and midshipmen are subject to automatic review by the Courts of Criminal Appeals. *Id.*

[19] 10 USC. § 866(c).

[20] *See* 10 USC. § 941.

[21] 10 USC. § 942(b) ("Each judge of [The CAAF] shall be appointed from civilian life by the President, by and with the advice and consent of the Senate....").

[22] 10 USC. § 867(a)(3).

[23] 10 USC. § 867(a)(1),(2).

[24] 10 USC. § 867(c).

[25] 526 US 529 (1999).

[26] *Id.* at 532-33.

[27] *Id.* at 534-36.

[28] *Id.* at 536.

[29] 28 USC. § 1259 (2008).

[30] 28 USC. § 1254(1).

[31] Weiss v. United States, 510 US 163, 177-81 (1994) (holding that lack of fixed terms for military court judges does not violate Fifth Amendment due process guarantees).

[32] *Id.*

[33] 60 M.J. 198, 205 (C.A.A.F. 2004).

[34] *Id.* at 199.

[35] 539 US 558 (2003).

[36] *Marcum*, 60 M.J. at 205.

[37] *Id.*

[38] *Id.* at 206.

[39] 128 S. Ct. 2641 (2008).

[40] *Kennedy*, Docket No. 07-343, Order September 8, 2008.

[41] Kennedy, 128 S. Ct. at 2645.

[42] *Id.* at 2657-58. For more information on Kennedy v. Louisiana, see CRS Report RS22844, *Capital Punishment:Constitutionality for Non-Homicide Crimes Such as Child Rape*, by Alison M. Smith.

[43] *Kennedy*, Docket No. 07-343, Petition for Rehearing.

[44] *Kennedy*, Denial of Petition for Rehearing, 129 S. Ct. 1, 2 (2009).

[45] 52 M.J. 504 (N-M. Ct. Crim. App. 1999), *rev'd*, 53 M.J. (C.A.A.F. 2000), *cert. denied*, 532 US 919 (2001), *remanded to* 65 M.J. 639 (N-M. Ct. Crim. App. 2006), *vacated*, 66 M.J. 15 (C.A.A.F. 2008), *cert. denied*, 129 S. Ct. 69 (2008), *vacated*, 2009 WL 4691176 (N-M. Ct. Crim. App. 2009).

[46] Brief of Petitioner-Appellant, United States v. Stevenson, No. 07-1397 (C.A.A.F. February 14, 2008).

[47] Brief for the United States in Opposition, United States v. Stevenson, No. 07-1397 (C.A.A.F. February 14, 2008).

[48] 28 USC. § 1259(3).

[49] *Stevenson*, 66 M.J. at 16-17.

[50] *Id.*

[51] *Id.* at 16.

[52] Brief of Petitioner-Appellant at i.

[53] Brief for the United States in Opposition at 7-10.

[54] *Id.*

[55] 129 S. Ct. 69 (2008).

[56] Equal Justice for Our Military Act of 2009, H.R. 569, 111th Cong. (2009); Equal Justice for Our Military Personnel Act of 2009, S. 357, 111th Cong. (2009) (The bills, as introduced, are identical to bills introduced in the 110th Congress: Equal Justice for United States Military Personnel Act of 2007, S. 2052, 110th Cong. (2008); Equal Justice for Our Military Act of 2007, H.R. 3174, 110th Cong. (2008). During the 110th Congress, the House passed the measure by voice vote, and Senator Leahy reported the Senate version after approval by the Senate Judiciary Committee. *See* 154 Cong. Rec. H10264 (daily ed. Sept. 27, 2008); 154 Cong. Rec. S8479 (daily ed. Sept. 12, 2008)).

[57] *Id.*

[58] 155 Cong. Rec. S1125 (daily ed. Jan. 30, 2009) (statement of Sen. Feinstein on behalf of herself, Senator Specter, and Senator Feingold).

[59] *Id.*

[60] US Congress, House Committee on the Judiciary, *Equal Justice for our Military Act of 2010*, report to accompany H.R. 569, 111th Cong., 2nd sess., July 15, 2010, H.Rept. 111-547 (Washington: GPO, 2010).

[61] *Id.* at 2.
[62] *Id.*
[63] *Id.*
[64] *Marcum*, 60 M.J. at 207-208.
[65] *Id.*

In: Jurisdiction ISBN: 978-1-62081-429-1
Editors: A. Stewart and D. Washington 

*Chapter 5*

# THE COPYRIGHT REGISTRATION REQUIREMENT AND FEDERAL COURT JURISDICTION: A LEGAL ANALYSIS OF *REED ELSEVIER, INC. V. MUCHNICK*[*]

***Brian T. Yeh***

## SUMMARY

Although an author need not register his or her work with the US Copyright Office to obtain copyright protection, registration is a statutory prerequisite to bringing suit for infringement of the copyright, as mandated by 17 USC. §411(a).

The question in *Reed Elsevier, Inc. v. Muchnick* is whether this section of the Copyright Act restricts the subject-matter jurisdiction of the federal courts over copyright infringement claims involving unregistered works.

The plaintiffs in *Reed Elsevier*, consisting of individual authors and trade groups representing authors, brought a class action lawsuit against several publishers when those publishers licensed the authors' articles for print publication but failed to secure an additional license to reproduce them electronically. The Supreme Court had earlier affirmed the plaintiffs' right to control electronic reproduction of their copyrighted works in its 2001 opinion *New York Times, Co. v. Tasini*.

---

[*] This is an edited, reformatted and augmented version of Congressional Research Service, Publication No. R40944, dated March 18, 2010.

After this opinion, the district court in *Reed Elsevier* referred the parties to mediation. After more than three years of negotiations, the parties reached an $18 million agreement that sorted the plaintiffs into three categories based, in part, on whether or not their copyrights had been registered. The settlement assigned a different damages formula to each category, with owners of registered copyrights receiving more than owners whose copyrights were unregistered.

Several freelance authors who fell within "Category C" (composed of unregistered copyrights) objected to the settlement agreement, arguing that the settlement was unfair and inadequate because they were paid too little. Proponents of the settlement responded that "Category C" claimants were treated fairly because, as owners of unregistered copyrights, they would normally be barred from bringing infringement suits at all under 17 USC. §411(a). The district court granted final class certification and approved the settlement in September of 2005.

The objectors appealed the district court's decision to the US Court of Appeals for the Second Circuit. Before oral argument, the Second Circuit asked the parties to address whether the district court had subject-matter jurisdiction over claims concerning the infringement of unregistered copyrights, or whether §411(a) restricted the court's jurisdiction.

Both the authors and publishers argued that §411(a) is not jurisdictional in nature. However, a divided panel of the Second Circuit disagreed, holding that the requirement of copyright registration prior to an infringement suit is jurisdictional and therefore, because many of the plaintiff's copyrights were unregistered, the district court lacked the power to certify the class and approve the settlement. The publishers appealed the appellate court's decision to the US Supreme Court.

In a unanimous decision issued on March 2, 2010, the US Supreme Court reversed the judgment of the Second Circuit panel. The Court characterized the Copyright Act's registration requirement as a claim-processing rule rather than a jurisdictional condition. Therefore, a copyright holder's failure to satisfy the statutory registration requirement does *not* deprive a federal court of jurisdiction to adjudicate his copyright infringement claim. While the Supreme Court held that the *Reed Elsevier* district court possesses the authority to approve the settlement between the authors and the publishers, the Court offered no opinion on the fairness, resonableness, or adequacy of the settlement.

On remand, the court of appeals must now consider the settlement's merits and decide whether to uphold the district court's approval of the settlement. The Supreme Court also expressly declined to decide whether §411(a) is a *mandatory* precondition to suit that district courts may or should enforce *sua sponte* by dismissing copyright infringement claims that involve unregistered works.

# BACKGROUND

Copyright is the exclusive right to reproduce, distribute, perform, display, and otherwise exploit an "original work of authorship," such as certain literary, dramatic, musical, or other artistic works.[1] Copyright protection is secured automatically when the work is created, or "fixed in any tangible medium of expression."[2] Although an author need not register his or her work with the US Copyright Office to obtain copyright protection, registration does come with several advantages. For instance, registration is necessary before a plaintiff may file an infringement suit,[3] and if registration is made within three months after publication of a work, the court may award the plaintiff statutory damages and attorney's fees rather than actual damages and profits alone.[4]

A copyright owner's exclusive right to reproduce and distribute his or her work was the subject of litigation in a 2001 Supreme Court case, *New York Times Co. v. Tasini.*[5] In *Tasini*, six freelance authors who had contributed articles to several publications, including *The New York Times*, *Newsday*, and *Time*, sued when the publishers licensed rights to copy and sell the articles to electronic databases such as Lexis/Nexis. The publishers argued that, because their magazines and newspapers were collective works composed of the authors' individual articles, section 201(c) of the Copyright Act permitted them to reproduce and distribute the articles as part of a "revision" of those collective works.[6] The Supreme Court disagreed. It held that the Copyright Act does not permit publishers to reproduce freelance works electronically when they lack specific authorization to do so, effectively requiring publishers to obtain a separate license from the author if they wish to electronically reproduce written works.[7] As a consequence of *Tasini,* many freelance works were removed from the electronic databases.[8]

Shortly after the Court decided *Tasini,* three preexisting class action infringement suits, which had been suspended pending the decision, were activated and consolidated in the US District Court for the Southern District of New York. A fourth, nearly identical action was coordinated with that consolidated action. Together, these claims comprise the litigation discussed in this report.[9]

Like the *Tasini* case, *Reed Elsevier v. Muchnick* is a class action lawsuit. Class actions allow one or more named plaintiffs to sue on behalf of a larger group of people when joining all members of the group would be impracticable; the members of the group raise similar claims, which present common issues of law or fact; and the named plaintiffs fairly and adequately protect the interests of other class members.[10] Litigation may proceed only after the court has certified the class,[11] and even settlement or voluntary dismissal of the suit requires the court's approval.[12] Any class member may object to a settlement proposal, but, once made, the objection may only be withdrawn with the court's permission.[13]

## The District Court's Opinion

The plaintiffs in *Reed Elsevier* consist of individual authors and trade groups representing authors who produced written works for certain publishers on a freelance basis.[14] The publishers had licensed the articles from the freelance authors for print publication but later reproduced the articles in their electronic databases without compensating or otherwise obtaining the consent of the authors. Based on their copyrights in the freelance works, the plaintiffs brought suit against the publishers and the electronic database services for copyright infringement.[15]

After the *Tasini* decision had affirmed the plaintiffs' right to control electronic reproduction of their works, the district court referred the parties to mediation.[16] In 2005, after more than three years of negotiations, the parties reached an agreement that sorted plaintiffs' claims into three groups for compensation purposes.[17]

Category A claims concerned copyrights that were eligible for statutory damages and attorney's fees under the Copyright Act.[18] Category B claims concerned copyrights that qualified for actual damages only.[19] Category C claims, by far the most numerous, largely involved copyrights that were unregistered, and therefore their owners were precluded from bringing individual suits for damages of any sort.[20]

The settlement assigned a damages formula to each type of claim. Category A claimants received a flat fee. Category B claimants received the greater of either a flat fee or a percentage of the original price of the work. Category C claimants also received the greater of either a flat fee or a percentage of the original price of the work. However, if the cost of all claims (plus the cost of notice, administration, and attorney's fees) exceeded $18 million, then the amount paid to Category C claimants was reduced—potentially to zero—before the claims of Category A and B claimants were affected. This feature was called the "C-reduction."[21] In return for financial compensation, the plaintiffs agreed to release all past, present, and future claims against the defendants related to their articles' appearance in electronic databases.[22]

Having reached an agreement, the plaintiffs and defendants moved the district court for class certification and settlement approval. Objectors opposed the motion on the ground that the settlement was inadequate and unfair to Category C claimants because they were paid little and singled out for reduction if the total claims exceeded $18 million. Objectors also maintained that the disparate treatment of Category C claimants illustrated that the named plaintiffs, who each possessed at least some registered copyrights, did not adequately represent those absent class members who possessed only unregistered copyrights. The defendants responded that Category C claimants were adequately represented and treated fairly because they would otherwise have been unable to bring actions for infringement at all under 17 USC. §411(a) because their copyrights were unregistered.[23]

After prolonged proceedings, the district court granted final class certification and final settlement approval in September 2005. Objectors appealed, again challenging the settlement's fairness and the adequacy of the named plaintiffs' representation.[24]

## THE SECOND CIRCUIT'S OPINION

Before hearing oral argument, the Second Circuit Court of Appeals "became concerned that the District Court and the parties had passed over a nettlesome jurisdictional question" and *sua sponte* ordered the parties to address "whether the District Court had subject-matter jurisdiction over claims concerning the infringement of unregistered copyrights."[25] Due to their mutual interest in achieving class certification and settlement approval at this stage, both plaintiffs and defendants argued that the Copyright Act's registration requirement is not jurisdictional in nature.[26] They contended that, if a plaintiff brings a single claim based on a registered copyright, the district court acquires jurisdiction over any and all related copyright claims, even if those other claims arise from unregistered copyrights. They also argued that jurisdiction in this case was proper because the named plaintiffs' works were registered.[27]

A divided panel of the Second Circuit disagreed. The majority opinion first observed that Congress provides federal courts with only limited subject-matter jurisdiction.[28] District courts derive their jurisdiction in copyright actions from two sections of Title 28 of the US Code, §1331 and § 1338. The first is a general grant of original jurisdiction over civil actions arising under federal law, and the second provides courts with a more specific grant of original jurisdiction over copyright infringement cases. However, the appellate court asserted that Congress has supplemented these basic jurisdictional grants with a separate statutory section— §411(a) of the Copyright Act (17 USC.§411(a)), which "limits a district court's subject-matter jurisdiction to claims arising from *registered* copyrights only."[29]

Relying on its opinions in *Well-Made Toy Mfg. Corp. v. Goffa Intl. Corp.*[30] and *Morris v. Bus. Concepts, Inc.*[31] and distinguishing the Supreme Court's ruling in *Eberhart v. United States*,[32] the appellate court held that the requirement of copyright registration prior to an infringement suit is jurisdictional[33] and that the phrase "copyright claim" referred to each claim within a purported class.[34] Thus, because many of the plaintiffs' copyrights were unregistered, the Second Circuit held that the district court lacked the authority to certify the class and, as a result, lacked jurisdiction to approve the settlement. It also held that this "jurisdictional defect" precluded supplemental jurisdiction[35] under 28 USC. §1367(a) as well.[36]

Judge Walker dissented, arguing that, although the Second Circuit had labeled §411(a) as jurisdictional in the past, the Supreme Court's ruling in *Eberhart*, which encouraged lower courts to "more carefully distinguish between true jurisdictional bars and claim-processing rules that may be waived," merited a re-evaluation of the copyright registration requirement.[37] Categorizing §411(a) as an "enforcement mechanism" rather than a "rights-creating statute"[38] and relying on Second Circuit precedent that "not all members of a settlement-only class need to possess a valid cause of action under the applicable law,"[39] he concluded that "the fact that some of the otherwise presumably valid copyrights have not been registered is an insufficient basis for undoing this class-action settlement."[40]

## ARGUMENTS BEFORE THE US SUPREME COURT

On March 2, 2009, the US Supreme Court granted certiorari to review the case on the following question: "Does 17 USC. §411(a) restrict the subject-matter jurisdiction of the federal courts over copyright infringement actions?"[41]

17 USC. §411(a) reads as follows:

> [N]o civil action for infringement of the copyright in any United States work shall be instituted until preregistration or registration of the copyright claim has been made in accordance with this title. In any

> case, however, where the deposit, application, and fee required for registration have been delivered to the Copyright Office in proper form and registration has been refused, the applicant is entitled to institute a civil action for infringement if notice thereof, with a copy of the complaint, is served on the Register of Copyrights. The Register may, at his or her option, become a party to the action with respect to the issue of registrability of the copyright claim by entering an appearance within sixty days after such service, but the Register's failure to become a party shall not deprive the court of jurisdiction to determine that issue.

Petitioners in the case (Reed Elsevier et al.) argued that the §411(a) registration requirement is a mandatory prerequisite to suit, not a restriction on the court's jurisdiction.[42] Drawing on the text, structure, legislative history, and purpose of the statute,[43] they argued that Congress never intended the registration requirement to be jurisdictional and that circuit courts interpreting it thus had failed to implement the "bright line" test articulated by the Supreme Court in its 2006 decision *Arbaugh v. Y&H Corp.*[44] Even if §411(a) is jurisdictional, petitioners argued that the restriction applies only to instituting actions, not settling them, because jurisdiction over an action generally extends to approving settlements that release claims the court lacked authority to try.[45] They warned that, if the Second Circuit's "drive-by"[46] jurisdictional characterization of §411(a) were allowed to stand, it would thwart "the ability of parties to reach negotiated resolutions of their disputes involving unregistered works" and leave "the nation's electronic databases and archives ... permanently depleted."[47]

Respondents (Pogrebin et al. and Irvin Muchnick et al.) advanced similar arguments, stating that §411(a) is not a bar to jurisdiction but rather a claim-processing rule, a prerequisite to suit that could be enforced or waived by the defendants.[48] As support, respondents cited several circuit court opinions in which the jurisdiction requirement was waived or relaxed and therefore treated "in a manner fundamentally inconsistent with its being subject-matter jurisdictional."[49] They also argued that, even if the district court had lacked original subject-matter jurisdiction over the case, it had supplemental jurisdiction because the claims of the Category-C authors with unregistered copyrights arose out of the same case or controversy as the claims of the Category-A and B authors whose copyrights were registered.[50]

The United States, as amicus curiae, also supported vacatur of the Second Circuit's judgment. Like petitioners, the US argued that §411(a) does not limit a federal courts' subject-matter jurisdiction, but rather serves as a mandatory prerequisite to suit that should be strictly enforced when raised by a party.[51] The US argued that, while district courts should ordinarily enforce §411(a) *sua sponte* even if the defendant did not move to dismiss on those grounds, once the case has reached the court of appeals, the district court has already expended significant resources, so insisting on a rigid application of §411(a) would waste judicial resources.[52] Therefore, according to the US, non-compliance with the registration requirement in this case provided no basis for vacating the district court's judgment.[53]

With both petitioners and respondents advocating the same outcome—that the Supreme Court overturn the Second Circuit's ruling—an unusual situation arose in which no party argued for the Court to affirm the judgment below. As a result, the Court appointed Professor Deborah Jones Merritt to serve as amicus curiae in support of the Second Circuit's judgment. According to Professor Merritt, not only does the plain language of §411(a) clearly restrict the subject-matter jurisdiction of federal courts,[54] but courts, legislators, and scholars have traditionally interpreted §411(a) as being jurisdictional.[55] Furthermore, she argued that §411(a) serves such vital public purposes as supporting a public record of copyright claims, shielding federal courts from burdensome litigation, protecting defendants from frivolous lawsuits, and supplying the Library of Congress collections.[56] Next, she argued that the integrity of the judicial process precludes the parties from waiving §411(a) because both parties invoked the jurisdictional bar before the district court to defend the fairness of their settlement, which rewarded the owners of registered copyrights at the expense of unregistered copyright owners.[57] Finally, Professor Merritt argued that neither a special rule for settlement nor the supplemental jurisdiction act cured this jurisdictional defect because (1) courts must have jurisdiction over class actions in order to terminate the claims of absent class members and (2) the many authors and databases involved in this lawsuit did not constitute a single case or controversy.[58]

The Computer and Communications Industry Association (CCIA) also provided an amicus brief in support of the Second Circuit's judgment. Echoing Professor Merritt's arguments, the CCIA cast the registration requirement as a necessary protection for Internet service providers, noting that, "[w]hen every blog and tweet might be protectable under copyright, the registration requirement dramatically reduces technology companies' potential exposure to copyright infringement claims."[59]

CCIA argued that the Second Circuit's opinion was correctly decided[60] and that the petitioners' writ of certoriari should be dismissed on two grounds.

First, there was no case or controversy before the court because petitioners themselves argued in the lower courts that §411(a) was jurisdictional in nature.[61] Second, circuit courts were in agreement that §411(a) limits federal courts' subject-matter jurisdiction; therefore, there was no circuit split, the traditional grounds on which the Supreme Court grants certiorari.[62] For these reasons, CCIA urged that the Supreme Court dismiss the petitioners' writ.

The Supreme Court heard oral argument in *Reed Elsevier* on October 7, 2009.[63]

## THE SUPREME COURT'S OPINION

On March 2, 2010, the US Supreme Court unanimously reversed the judgment of the US Court of Appeals for the Second Circuit. In an opinion authored by Justice Thomas, the Court ruled that while the Copyright Act's registration requirement is a precondition to filing a claim for infringement, §411(a) does *not* limit or deprive a federal court of subject-matter jurisdiction to adjudicate copyright infringement claims involving unregistered works.[64] Consequently, the Court held that the district court had the authority to certify the class and to approve the settlement between the freelance authors, publishers, and electronic databases.[65]

At the beginning of its opinion, the Supreme Court first noted that "subject-matter jurisdiction refers to the courts' statutory or constitutional power to adjudicate the case," and that jurisdictional statutes "speak to the power of the court rather than the rights or obligations of parties."[66]

Some statutory requirements are not jurisdictional conditions, but rather "claim-processing rules" or elements of a cause of action, the Court explained.[67]

To help federal courts distinguish between true jurisdictional conditions and nonjurisdictional claim-processing rules or elements of a claim, the Supreme Court referred to the "general approach" it had articulated in its 2006 decision, *Arbaugh v. Y & H Corp.*:

> If the Legislature clearly states that a threshold limitation on a statute's scope shall count as jurisdictional, then courts and litigants will be duly instructed and will not be left to wrestle with the issue. But when Congress does not rank a statutory limitation on coverage as jurisdictional, courts should treat the restriction as nonjurisdictional in character.[68]

Arbaugh involved a sexual harassment case brought by an employee against an employer under Title VII of the Civil Rights Act of 1964. For a Title VII action, Congress specifically limited the definition of "employer" to include only those having 15 or more employees.[69] The Arbaugh Court held that this numerical qualification contained within Title VII's definition of "employer" was a substantive element of the claim for relief that did not affect federal court subject-matter jurisdiction.[70]

In reaching this conclusion, the Arbaugh Court had observed that Title VII's employee numerosity requirement did not "clearly state[]" that it is jurisdictional; furthermore, no prior Supreme Court case involving Title VII claims had suggested that the numerosity requirement imposed a jurisdictional limit.[71] In addition, the employee numerosity requirement is located in a statutory provision that is separate from Title VII's jurisdiction-granting section.

The Reed Elsevier Court found the Arbaugh precedent controlling with respect to §411(a) of the Copyright Act. As in Arbaugh, the Court failed to find that Congress explicitly labeled §411(a)'s registration requirement as jurisdictional.[72] In reaching this conclusion, the Court rejected Professor Merritt's argument that the mere presence of the word "jurisdiction" in the last sentence of §411(a) indicates that Congress ranked the requirement as jurisdictional.

The Court asserted that the statutory reference to "jurisdiction" was Congress' deliberate intent to make "it clear that a federal court plainly has adjudicatory authority to determine 'that issue'... i.e., the issue of registrability—regardless whether the Register is a party to the infringement suit."[73] Furthermore, the Court observed, §411(a) is located in Title 17 of the US Code (the Copyright Act), separate from statutory provisions (in Title 28) that grant federal courts subject-matter jurisdiction over copyright infringement actions; neither of those statutory provisions (28 USC. §§1331 and 1338) "condition its jurisdictional grant on whether copyright holders have registered their works before suing for infringement."[74] The Court also pointed out that §411(a) contains "congressionally authorized exceptions" to the requirement for registration prior to filing an infringement suit:

> [M]ost significantly, §411(a) expressly *allows* courts to adjudicate infringement claims involving unregistered works in three circumstances: where the work is not a US work, where the infringement claim concerns rights of attribution and integrity under §

106A, or where the holder attempted to register the work and registration was refused.[75]

The Court argued that "[i]t would be at least unusual to ascribe jurisdictional significance to a condition subject to these sorts of exceptions."[76] Finally, the Court cited several of its earlier decisions that had treated as nonjurisdictional other types of statutory prerequisites or threshold requirements that plaintiffs must satisfy before initiating a lawsuit.[77]

In applying the *Arbaugh* precedent to the matter at hand, the *Reed Elsevier* Court attempted to distinguish its 2007 decision, *Bowles v. Russell.*[78] The *Bowles* case examined a statutory provision that required parties in a federal civil action to file a notice of appeal within 30 days of the judgment being appealed. Although Congress did not explicitly label the statutory condition as jurisdictional, the *Bowles* Court noted that Supreme Court precedents have historically treated the limitation for taking an appeal as jurisdictional and thus, the statutory condition may be "properly ranked as jurisdictional absent an express designation."[79]

The *Reed Elsevier* Court explained that *Bowles* "stands for the proposition that context, including this Court's interpretation of similar provisions in many years past, is relevant to whether a statute ranks a requirement as jurisdictional."[80] Here, §411(a)'s registration requirement does not implicate subject-matter jurisdiction because it is a condition that is more analogous to the *Arbaugh* employee numerosity requirement than the *Bowles* statutory time limit.[81]

The Court rejected Professor Merritt's argument that §411(a) should be construed as jurisdictional in order to promote policy goals and "important congressional objectives" underlying copyright registration.[82] The Court also declined to affirm on estoppel grounds the appellate court's judgment, as Professor Merritt had urged. The Court noted that the judicial estoppel doctrine usually applies when a party has successfully persuaded a court to accept that party's earlier position, "so that judicial acceptance of an inconsistent position in a later proceeding would create the perception that either the first or the second court was misled."[83] Here, the parties' assertion that §411(a) was jurisdictional in defending or negotiating the settlement agreement was a position that followed existing precedent in the Second Circuit; "more importantly, in approving the settlement, the District Court did not adopt petitioners' interpretation of § 411(a) as jurisdictional."[84]

In the appellate court, the petitioners argued that §411(a) did not restrict the district court's subject-matter jurisdiction—an argument that the Second

Circuit rejected. Therefore, the Supreme Court's adoption of the petitioners' arguments would not create "inconsistent court determinations" in their favor; thus, the circumstances supporting estoppel do not exist.[85]

Finally, the Supreme Court expressed no opinion on the fairness, resonableness, or adequacy of the settlement. The merits of the settlement along with the objections to it will now be considered by the court of appeals. The Supreme Court also expressly declined to decide whether §411(a) is a *mandatory* precondition to suit that district courts may or should enforce *sua sponte* by dismissing copyright infringement claims that involve unregistered works.[86] Thus, this question remains open for lower courts to consider.

## Concurrence

Justice Ginsburg wrote a concurrence, joined by Justices Stevens and Breyer, in which she agreed with the judgment of the Court that §411(a) should be treated as a precondition to filing a copyright infringement claim that does not restrict a federal court's subject-matter jurisdiction. However, she pointed out the "undeniable tension" between the *Arbaugh* and *Bowles* precedents and then offered her understanding of those opinions in an attempt to reconcile the rulings.[87]

First, she stated that a unanimous *Arbaugh* Court had announced a "readily administrable bright line"[88] rule that federal courts would apply in deciding what statutory conditions qualify as jurisdictional and what does not—that is, such conditions "are only jurisdictional if Congress says so."[89] Yet just one year after *Arbaugh,* a "sharply divided" *Bowles* Court "moved in a different direction" by finding the statutory time limit for filing a notice of appeal to be jurisdictional simply because Supreme Court precedents had long considered it to be so.[90]

Justice Ginsburg offered an approach to reconciling *Bowles* and *Arbaugh* by suggesting that *Bowles* relied on longstanding decisions *of the Supreme Court* that have been left undisturbed by Congress.[91] Here, *Arbaugh*'s bright line rule supports the conclusion that §411(a) is nonjurisdictional because it does not speak in jurisdictional terms or refer to the jurisdiction of district courts, Justice Ginsburg noted. Although there may be "over 200 opinions that characterize §411(a) as jurisdictional" that comprise "a century's worth of precedent,"[92] *Bowles* does not apply to the Copyright Act's registration requirement, Justice Ginsburg argued, because those opinions are from the lower courts, and not one is from the Supreme Court.[93]

## CONCLUDING OBSERVATIONS

The *Reed Elsevier* case is now remanded to the US Court of Appeals for the Second Circuit to consider the settlement's merits and the objections to the settlement's approval. If the appellate court upholds the district court's approval of the settlement, the freelance authors will receive financial compensation and the electronic databases will be able to restore the publications to their archives. However, the appellate court may pay particular attention to the objections to the settlement's proposed damages formula, as suggested by Judge Walker's dissent to the Second Circuit's ruling in this case:

> On the merits, the failure to create a sub-class consisting of those members holding primarily "C-class" claims, and separate representation for those members, is a serious problem in my view, because the named representatives hold more "A-class" and "B-class" claims than most class members, and thus have an incentive to favor holders of A- and B-class claims over holders of primarily C-class claims. ... Objectors point out that such favoritism may have occurred- as the so-called "C-reduction" ... ensures that C-class claim holders are paid little or perhaps nothing.[94]

The Supreme Court's opinion in *Reed Elsevier* not only affects the particular settlement at issue, but has implications for copyright holders in future infringement cases. First, this case suggests that copyright holders who have not registered their works may still be able to participate in copyright infringement settlements and class action lawsuits involving both registered and unregistered works, despite their lack of compliance with §411(a). However, the Court leaves open the possibility for district courts to dismiss, *sua sponte*, copyright infringement claims involving an unregistered work. On the other hand, the decision also reaffirms the authority of federal courts to consider (and approve) a copyright infringement class action settlement involving both registered and unregistered works.

Beyond its impact in copyright law litigation, *Reed Elsevier* also helps clarify the Court's jurisprudence on subject-matter jurisdiction of federal courts. The case reaffirms *Arbaugh*'s clear statement rule as the primary test for statutory limitations, while the concurrence attempts to confine *Bowles* to only those situations where the Supreme Court has historically treated the limitation as jurisdictional.

## End Notes

[1] *See* 17 USC. §106; *see also* US Copyright Office: Copyright Basics, *at* http://www.copyright.gov/circs/circ1.pdf, and CRS Report RS22801, *General Overview of US Copyright Law*, by Brian T. Yeh.

[2] 17 USC. §102(a).

[3] *See* 17 USC. §411(a).

[4] *See* 17 USC. §412.

[5] 533 US 483 (2001). For more information on this decision, see CRS Report RS20964, *New York Times Co. v. Tasini: The US Supreme Court Affirms "Authorial" Rights in Copyright*, by Robin Jeweler.

[6] *Id.* at 484.

[7] *See* New York Times Co. v. Tasini, 533 US 483 (2001).

[8] Adam Liptak, *Justices Reinstate Settlement With Writers,* N.Y. TIMES, Mar. 2, 2010, at B10. The articles at issue in the case were published between 1980 and 1995. Since 1995, the New York Times and other publishers have required freelance writers to grant them electronic reproduction rights in their works in addition to print publication rights. *Id.; see also Tasini,* 533 US at 522 (Stevens, J., dissenting).

[9] *See* Muchnick v. Thomson Corp. (In re Literary Works in Electronic Databases Copyright Litigation), 509 F.3d 116, 118 (2d Cir. 2007).

[10] Fed. R. Civ. P. 23(a).

[11] Fed. R. Civ. P. 23(c)(1)(A).

[12] Fed. R. Civ. P. 23(e).

[13] Fed. R. Civ. P. 23(e)(5).

[14] *See In re Literary Works in Electronic Databases Copyright Litigation*, 509 F.3d at 118-19.

[15] *Id.* at 119.

[16] *Id.*

[17] *Id.* at 120.

[18] *See id.* (citing 17 USC. §412).

[19] *See id.*

[20] *See id.*

[21] *Id.*

[22] See Brief for the United States as Amicus Curiae Supporting Vacatur and Remand at 8, Reed Elsevier, Inc. v. Muchnick, No. 08-103 (550 US ___, March 2, 2010).

[23] *In re Literary Works in Electronic Databases Copyright Litigation,* 509 F.3d at 120.

[24] *Id.*

[25] *Id.*

[26] *Id.* at 122.

[27] *Id.* at 123.

[28] *Id.* at 121.

[29] *Id.* at 122 (emphasis added).

[30] 354 F. 3d 112 (2d Cir. 2003).

[31] 259 F.3d 65 (2d Cir. 2001).

[32] 546 US 12 (2005).

[33] *In re Literary Works in Electronic Databases Copyright Litigation,* 509 F.3d at 121.

[34] *Id.* at 125.

[35] Supplemental jurisdiction is "a court's jurisdiction to hear and determine a claim over which it would not otherwise have jurisdiction, because the claim arises from the same transaction or

occurrence as another claim that is properly before the court." BLACK'S LAW DICTIONARY (8th ed. 2004).

[36] *In re Literary Works in Electronic Databases Copyright Litigation*, 509 F.3d at 127.

[37] *Id.* at 128 (Walker, J., dissenting).

[38] *Id.* at 130.

[39] *Id.* at 128 (referencing Lerner v. Fleet Bank, 318 F.3d 113, 125-26 (2d Cir.2003) (holding that, in a RICO class action suit, the district court could exercise supplemental jurisdiction over plaintiffs' state-law claims despite the fact that certain members of the plaintiff class lacked RICO standing)).

[40] *Id.*

[41] Reed Elsevier, Inc. v. Muchnick, 129 S.Ct. 1523 (2009).

[42] *See* Brief for Petitioners at 15, Reed Elsevier, Inc. v. Muchnick, No. 08-103 (550 US ___, March 2, 2010).

[43] *See id.* at 23-37.

[44] *Id.* at 40-45 (citing Arbaugh v. Y & H Corp., 546 US 500, 516 (2006)).

[45] *See id.* at 45-48.

[46] Id. at 40 (citing Steel Co. v. Citizens for a Better Env't, 523 US 83, 91 (1998)).

[47] Id. at 3.

[48] *See* Brief for Respondents Pogrebin et al. in Support of Petitioners at 5, Reed Elsevier, Inc. v. Muchnick, No. 08-103 (550 US ___, March 2, 2010); *see also* Brief for the Muchnick Respondents at 18-32, Reed Elsevier, Inc. v. Muchnick, No. 08-103 (550 US ___, March 2, 2010).

[49] Brief for Respondents Pogrebin et al. at 5.

[50] *See id.* at 18-23; s*ee also* Brief for the Muchnick Respondents at 36-44.

[51] *See* Brief for the United States as Amicus Curiae Supporting Vacatur and Remand at 20-25, Reed Elsevier, Inc. v. Muchnick, No. 08-103 (550 US ___, March 2, 2010).

[52] *See id.* at 25-31.

[53] *See id.* at 30.

[54] *See* Brief of Court-Appointed Amicus Curiae in Support of the Judgment Below at 17-26, Reed Elsevier, Inc. v. Muchnick, No. 08-103 (550 US ___, March 2, 2010).

[55] *See id.* at 26-44.

[56] *See id.* at 44-57. 17 USC. §407 requires copyright owners, within three months of publication, to deposit two copies of their work with the US Copyright Office for inclusion in the Library of Congress. This requirement ensures that the nation's public library contains copies of every work published in the United States. 17 USC. §407(a).

[57] *See* Brief of Court-Appointed Amicus Curiae at 57-65.

[58] *See id.* at 65-69.

[59] Brief for Amici Curiae Computer & Communications Industry Association and Netcoalition in Support of the Judgment Below at 3, Reed Elsevier, Inc. v. Muchnick, No. 08-103 (550 US ___, March 2, 2010).

[60] *See id.* at 23-35.

[61] *See id.* at 7-18.

[62] *See id.* at 18-23.

[63] Associate Justice Sonia Sotomayor recused herself from the case, leaving only eight of the nine justices to rule on the issue. Some observers speculated that Justice Sotomayor's recusal stems from either her 1997 ruling in the *Tasini* case as a federal judge in the Southern District of New York, or her position on the Second Circuit when the court, in 2008, refused to grant an *en banc* rehearing of *In re Literary Works in Electronic Databases Copyright*

*Litigation. See Eight Justice Court for Copyright Case,* SCOTUSBLOG, Sept. 4, 2009, *at* http://www.scotusblog.com/wp/eight-judge-courtfor-copyright

[64] Reed Elsevier, Inc. v. Muchnick, No. 08-103, slip op. at 1-2 (550 US ___, March 2, 2010).

[65] *Id.* at 15-16.

[66] *Id.* at 5 (citations and internal quotations omitted).

[67] *Id.* at 5-6.

[68] *Id.* at 6 (quoting *Arbaugh*, 546 US 500, 515-16 (2006)).

[69] *Arbaugh,* 546 US at 503.

[70] *Id.* at 515-16.

[71] *Reed Elsevier,* No. 08-103, slip op. at 7.

[72] *Id.* at 8.

[73] *Id.* at 8-9 (emphasis in original).

[74] *Id.* at 9.

[75] *Id.* at 10 (emphasis in original).

[76] *Id.*

[77] *Id.* at 10-11 (citing Zipes v. Trans World Airlines, Inc., 455 US 385 (1982), Woodford v. Ngo, 548 US 81 (2006), and Jones v. Bock, 549 US 199 (2007)).

[78] 551 US 205 (2007).

[79] *Reed Elsevier,* No. 08-103, slip op. at 13.

[80] *Id.* at 13.

[81] *Id.* at 13-14.

[82] *Id.* at 14 n.9.

[83] *Id.* at 15 (citation omitted).

[84] *Id.*

[85] *Id.*

[86] *Id.* at 16.

[87] *Reed Elsevier,* No. 08-103, slip op. at 1 (Ginsburg, J., concurring).

[88] *Id.* at 2 (quoting *Arbaugh,* 546 US at 515-516).

[89] *Id.* at 2-3 (quoting *Bowles,* 551 US at 217 (Souter, J., dissenting).

[90] *Id.* at 2.

[91] *Id.* (citation omitted) (emphasis added).

[92] *Id.* at 3.

[93] *Id.* at 3-4.

[94] *In re Literary Works in Electronic Databases Copyright Litigation*, 509 F.3d at 136 n.5 (Walker, J., dissenting).

In: Jurisdiction ISBN: 978-1-62081-429-1
Editors: A. Stewart and D. Washington 

*Chapter 6*

# JURISDICTION OVER CHALLENGES TO "LARGE" ORDERS UNDER FEDERAL CONTRACTS*

***Kate M. Manuel and Erika K. Lunder***

## SUMMARY

On December 31, 2011, President Obama signed the National Defense Authorization Act for FY2012. This act amends Title 41 of the United States Code to extend the Government Accountability Office's (GAO's) jurisdiction over protests involving "large" orders issued under civilian agency contracts and clarifies that protests of such orders may not be heard after September 30, 2016, if this jurisdiction is not reauthorized (P.L. 112-81, § 813). Title 41's provisions regarding the protests of "large" orders previously had a May 27, 2011, sunset date. However, the language of these provisions was such that GAO and the US Court of Federal Claims construed them to mean that they could hear protests of orders of any size issued under civilian agency contracts after May 27, 2011. These cases arose because of amendments that the Federal Acquisition Streamlining Act (FASA) of 1994 and the National Defense Authorization Act (NDAA) for FY2008 made to the Armed Services Procurement Act and the Federal Property and Administrative Services Act.

---

* This is an edited, reformatted and augmented version of Congressional Research Service, Publication No. R42049, dated January 17, 2012.

Before FASA was enacted, GAO, the federal courts, and procuring agencies had jurisdiction over protests alleging that agency conduct in the issuance of orders under federal contracts was arbitrary, capricious, an abuse of discretion, or otherwise not in accordance with the law. However, FASA limited this jurisdiction, barring all protests regarding the issuance of orders except those alleging that the order increased the scope, period, or maximum value of the underlying contract.

Later, the NDAA for FY2008 amended FASA to expand the grounds upon which the issuance of orders could be protested, authorizing GAO to hear protests of orders valued in excess of $10 million that did not increase the scope, period, or maximum value of the underlying contract. The NDAA for FY2008 also included a sunset provision, specifying that this "subsection" expired on May 27, 2011.

Executive branch agencies and many commentators construed this language to mean that GAO's jurisdiction over protests of "large" orders expired on May 27, 2011. However, GAO and, later, the Court of Federal Claims disagreed.

First, in *Technatomy Corporation*, GAO relied upon the statute's "plain meaning" to find that "subsection" meant the entirety of FASA's provisions regarding protests of orders, as amended, and not just the amendments made to these provisions by the NDAA for FY2008. According to GAO, what expired on May 27, 2011, were the limitations on its jurisdiction over protests that do not increase the scope, period, or maximum value of the underlying contract, as amended by the expansion of its jurisdiction to include protests of "large" orders.

Thus, it concluded that it may hear protests of orders of any size issued under civilian agency contracts, regardless of whether the protest alleges that the order increased the scope, period, or maximum value of the underlying contract. Later, in *Med Trends, Inc. v. United States*, the court similarly relied upon the "plain meaning" of FASA, as amended by the NDAA for FY2008.

However, the court also explicitly rejected the government's argument that the legislative history of the NDAA for FY2008 supported construing "subsection" to mean only those provisions of FASA granting GAO jurisdiction over protests of orders valued in excess of $10 million.

These decisions would have resulted in protests of orders under civilian agency contracts being treated differently than protests of similar orders under defense contracts, and could also have increased the number of bid protests.

The $111^{th}$ Congress (P.L. 111-383, § 825) had previously amended Title 10 of the United States Code, which governs the procurements of defense agencies, with language identical to that in P.L. 112-81.

## Introduction

This report discusses recent legislation and decisions by the Government Accountability Office (GAO) and the US Court of Federal Claims regarding jurisdiction over orders issued under civilian agency contracts. On December 31, 2011, President Obama signed legislation[1] that effectively overturned two recent decisions by GAO and the Court of Federal Claims finding that they have jurisdiction over protests challenging the issuance of task and delivery orders of any size under civilian agency contracts,[2] even if these orders do not increase the scope, period, or maximum value of the underlying contract.[3] Prior to these decisions, executive branch agencies and many commentators had construed the Federal Acquisition Streamlining Act (FASA) of 1994, as amended by the National Defense Authorization Act (NDAA) for FY2008, as authorizing only protests concerning the issuance of orders under civilian agency contracts that (1) increased the scope, period, or maximum value of the underlying contract or (2) were valued in excess of $10 million, as well as granting GAO temporary exclusive jurisdiction over protests involving the latter.[4] However, GAO and the court rejected this interpretation, finding that what expired on May 27, 2011, were limitations on their jurisdiction imposed by FASA, as amended by the NDAA for FY2008. Thus, they concluded that they and, potentially, procuring agencies had jurisdiction over protests of orders of any size issued under the contracts of civilian agencies, regardless of whether these orders increased the scope, period, or maximum value of the underlying contract.[5]

Had they not been overturned by Congress, these decisions would have resulted in protests of orders under civilian agency contracts being treated differently than protests of similar orders under defense contracts, and could also have increased the number of bid protests.

## FASA and Subsequent Amendments

The decisions by GAO and the Court of Federal Claims arose from questions regarding the meaning of certain provisions of FASA[6] and amendments made to it by the NDAA for FY2008[7] and the Ike Skelton NDAA for FY2011.[8] For various reasons, including agencies' use of detailed specifications to restrict competition and difficulties procuring commercial items during the Gulf War, by the early to mid-1990s, many Members of

Congress and commentators had become concerned that the federal procurement process was excessively cumbersome and time-consuming for both agencies and contractors.[9] FASA represented Congress's first attempt to respond to these concerns "by greatly streamlining and simplifying [the federal government's] buying practices."[10] FASA did so, in part, by explicitly recognizing "task and delivery order contracts,"[11] and by limiting contractors' ability to protest alleged improprieties in agencies' issuance of orders under task and delivery order (TO/DO) contracts, among other things. TO/DO contracts are contracts for services or goods, respectively, that do not "procure or specify a firm quantity of supplies (other than a minimum or maximum quantity)," but rather "provide[] for the issuance of orders for the delivery of supplies during the period of the contract."[12] Because the time of delivery and the quantity of goods or services to be delivered are not specified (outside of stated maximums or minimums) in TO/DO contracts, such contracts are sometimes referred to as indefinite delivery/indefinite quantity (ID/IQ) contracts.[13] TO/DO contracts are sometimes also described as single-award or multiple-award contracts, a designation based upon the number of firms—one or more than one, respectively—able to compete for task and delivery orders under the contract.[14] Before FASA was enacted, disappointed bidders and offerors could generally protest agency conduct in the award, or proposed award, of federal contracts that was "arbitrary, capricious, an abuse of discretion, or otherwise not in accordance with the law" before GAO, the federal courts, or procuring agencies.[15] GAO, in particular, had found that it had jurisdiction over protests regarding the issuance of orders under TO/DO contracts.[16]

Use of TO/DO contracts can greatly simplify the procurement process for federal agencies because agencies can issue orders to contractors holding the underlying TO/DO contract without complying with the requirements of the Competition in Contracting Act (CICA) of 1984, among other things.[17] This, in itself, can significantly reduce the time necessary for agencies to procure goods or services.[18] However, FASA further simplified the procurement process for federal agencies by limiting the ability of bidders or offerors to protest alleged improprieties or illegalities in the issuance of orders under TO/DO contracts.[19] In identical provisions codified in Titles 10 and 41 of the United States Code, FASA expressly prohibited protests challenging the issuance of orders except on certain narrow grounds:

> A protest is not authorized in connection with the issuance or proposed issuance of a task or delivery order except for a protest on

> the ground that the order increases the scope, period, or maximum value of the contract under which the order is issued.[20]

The provisions codified in Title 10 apply to the procurements of defense agencies, while those codified in Title 41 apply to the procurements of civilian agencies.

## National Defense Authorization Act for FY2008

By 2008, congressional and public concerns regarding federal procurement had shifted, largely because of alleged waste, fraud, and abuse in contracts supporting military, diplomatic, and reconstruction efforts in Iraq and Afghanistan.[21] Rather than viewing the federal procurement process as too burdensome and time-consuming, as they did when FASA was enacted, some Members of Congress and commentators now believed that agencies had used their authority under FASA and similar laws to evade the spirit, if not the letter, of competition and other requirements.[22] These concerns persisted notwithstanding a series of judicial and administrative decisions finding that GAO and the federal courts *could* exercise jurisdiction over certain protests involving the issuance of orders that did not increase the scope, period, or maximum value of the underlying contract.[23] In fact, the Acquisition Advisory Panel, chartered under Section 1423 of the Services Acquisition Reform Act (SARA) of 2003, explicitly recommended that contractors be able to protest the issuance of "large" orders that do not increase the scope, period, or maximum value of the underlying contract.[24]

Congress responded, in part, to these concerns when it enacted the NDAA for FY2008. This act amended FASA to promote competition for orders under TO/DO contracts by (1) prohibiting agencies from using single-award TO/DO contracts valued in excess of $103 million (including options) unless certain conditions are met,[25] and (2) specifying what constitutes a "fair opportunity to be considered" for orders valued in excess of $5 million.[26] In addition, the NDAA for FY2008 also expanded protesters' ability to challenge alleged improprieties or illegalities in the issuance of orders. Specifically, the NDAA for FY2008 amended FASA to read as follows:

> A protest is not authorized in connection with the issuance or proposed issuance of a task or delivery order except for —

> (A) a protest on the ground that the order increases the scope, period, or maximum value of the contract under which the order is issued; or
> (B) a protest of an order valued in excess of $10,000,000.[27]

The 2008 amendments further specified that GAO was to have exclusive jurisdiction over protests of orders valued in excess of $10 million that did not increase the scope, period, or maximum value of the underlying contract,[28] and that

> This subsection shall be in effect for three years, beginning on the date that is 120 days after January 28, 2008.[29]

Many commentators interpreted the word "subsection" here to refer to the provisions regarding GAO's exclusive jurisdiction over protests of orders valued in excess of $10 million because these provisions were added, along with the sunset clause, in 2008.[30] In addition, the legislative history of the 2008 amendments arguably indicated that Congress intended to temporarily authorize protests of "large" orders in order to gauge their effects on the procurement and protest processes before permanently authorizing such protests.[31]

## Ike Skelton National Defense Authorization Act for FY2011

Three years and 120 days after the enactment of the NDAA for FY2008 would have been May 27, 2011.[32] However, before this date arrived, the 111th Congress amended FASA's provisions regarding protests of orders issued under defense contracts to extend the sunset date and clarify that it applies only to GAO's exclusive jurisdiction over protests of "large" orders. Specifically, the Ike Skelton NDAA for FY2011 amended those provisions of FASA codified in Title 10 of the United States Code to read as follows:

> (1) A protest is not authorized in connection with the issuance or proposed issuance of a task or delivery order except for –
> (A) a protest on the ground that the order increases the scope, period, or maximum value of the contract under which the order is issued; or
> (B) a protest of an order valued in excess of $10,000,000.

(2) Notwithstanding section 3556 of title 31, the Comptroller General of the United States shall have exclusive jurisdiction of a protest authorized under paragraph (1)(B).
(3) *Paragraph (1)(B) and paragraph (2) of this subsection* shall not be in effect after September 30, 2016.[33]

The 111th Congress did not make similar changes to the provisions of FASA codified in Title 41 of the United States Code governing protests of orders under civilian agency contracts. Thus, the provisions in Title 41 differed slightly from those in Title 10 at the time when GAO and the Court of Federal Claims issued their decisions. When their decisions were issued, subsection (B)(3) in Title 41 stated that "*This subsection* shall be in effect for three years, beginning on the date that is 120 days after January 28, 2008,"[34] not "*Paragraph (1)(B) and paragraph (2) of this subsection* shall not be in effect after September 30, 2016."

## THE GAO AND COURT DECISIONS

In its June 14, 2011, decision in *Technatomy Corporation*, GAO found that it had jurisdiction over an order placed under a civilian agency contract that apparently did not expand the scope, period, or maximum value of the underlying contract.[35] The Department of Defense (DOD), which had issued the challenged order under a General Services Administration (GSA) contract, argued that because Congress had not extended the sunset date as to the orders of civilian agencies, GAO's jurisdiction to hear protests concerning task and delivery orders valued in excess of $10 million issued under civilian agency contracts expired on May 27, 2011.[36] GAO disagreed, because of the "plain meaning" of the relevant provisions of FASA.[37] GAO found that the word "subsection" in 41 USC. §4106(f)(3) "unambiguously refers" to the entirety of subsection (f), which governs protests of civilian agency orders generally, not just subsection (f)(2), which grants GAO jurisdiction over protests of "large" orders.[38] Based upon this interpretation of "subsection," GAO found that what expired in May 2011 were the limitations on its jurisdiction under FASA, as amended by the expansion of its jurisdiction under the NDAA for FY2008.[39] Thus, it concluded that, because of the expiration of these limitations, its jurisdiction "revert[ed] to that originally provided in CICA,"[40] and it could hear protests concerning orders of any value under civilian agency contracts, regardless of whether the order increased the scope, period, or maximum value of the underlying contract.[41]

Subsequently, in its August 19, 2011, decision in *Med Trends, Inc. v. United States*, the Court of Federal Claims also found that it had jurisdiction over protests of orders of any value issued under civilian agency contracts.[42] In so finding, the court rejected the government's argument that, "notwithstanding the clear language of the statute, the legislative history associated with the 2008 amendment makes clear that the grant of jurisdiction to GAO in 2008 was a short-term experiment."[43]

The court did so, in part, because it, like GAO, found that the word "subsection" referred to the entirety of FASA's provisions regarding protests of task and delivery orders issued under civilian agency contracts, not just those provisions regarding GAO's jurisdiction over "large" orders issued under civilian agency contracts.[44] Because it viewed this statutory text as "unambiguous," the court accorded no weight to a 2007 conference report expressing the conferees' view that the expiration of GAO's jurisdiction over "large" orders would provide "Congress with an opportunity to review the implementation of the provision and make any necessary adjustments."[45] It similarly declined to rely upon legislation introduced in the 112th Congress and accompanying committee reports that purportedly evidenced Congress's intent that the sunset date apply only to GAO's exclusive jurisdiction over protests of orders valued in excess of $10 million.[46]

Had the 112th Congress not enacted legislation extending the sunset date, these decisions would have resulted in protests of orders issued under civilian agency contracts being treated differently than protests of similar orders under defense contracts,[47] and could also have increased the number of bid protests.[48] The legislation also arguably resolves certain questions that had been raised about the authority of the Federal Acquisition Regulatory Council to promulgate an interim final regulation amending the Federal Acquisition Regulation (FAR) to provide that

> (i) No protest under Subpart 33.1 is authorized in connection with the issuance or proposed issuance of an order under a task-order contract or delivery-order contract, except for—
> (A) A protest on the grounds that the order increases the scope, period, or maximum value of the contract; or
> (B) A protest of an order valued in excess of $10 million. Protests of orders in excess of $10 million may only be filed with the

> Government Accountability Office, in accordance with the procedures at 33.104.
> (ii) *The authority to protest the placement of an order under this subpart expires* on September 30, 2016, for DoD, NASA and the Coast Guard (10 USC. 2304a(d) and 2304c(e)), and *on May 27, 2011, for other agencies* (41 USC. 4103(d) and 4106(f)).[49]

Both the meaning of this provision and the FAR Council's authority to promulgate such a regulation could have been in doubt, particularly after the decision by the Court of Federal Claims.[50] As amended, the regulation could have been construed to mean that neither protests of orders that allegedly increased the scope, period, or maximum value of the underlying contract, nor protests of orders valued in excess of $10 million, were authorized for civilian agency contracts.[51] However, such an interpretation could potentially have been found not to be entitled to deference under *Chevron USA., Inc. v. Natural Resources Defense Council, Inc.*[52] Under *Chevron*, courts generally defer to an agency's formal interpretation of a statute that the agency administers whenever the agency's interpretation is reasonable, and the statute has not removed the agency's discretion by compelling a particular disposition of the matter at issue. Agency interpretations are not granted such deference, though, when "Congress has directly spoken to the precise question at issue," and the agency's interpretation is at variance with the statutory language.[53]

## NATIONAL DEFENSE AUTHORIZATION ACT FOR FY2012

The NDAA for FY2012 amended Title 41 of the United States Code so that it reads like Title 10:

> (1) A protest is not authorized in connection with the issuance or proposed issuance of a task or delivery order except for –
> (A) a protest on the ground that the order increases the scope, period, or maximum value of the contract under which the order is issued; or
> (B) a protest of an order valued in excess of $10,000,000.
> (2) Notwithstanding section 3556 of title 31, the Comptroller General of the United States shall have exclusive jurisdiction of a protest authorized under paragraph (1)(B).

(3) *Paragraph (1)(B) and paragraph (2) of this subsection* shall not be in effect after September 30, 2016.[54]

Because of these amendments, and the amendments made to Title 10 in 2011, GAO and the Court of Federal Claims are unlikely to find that they have jurisdiction over orders that do not increase the scope, period, or maximum value of the underlying contracts after September 30, 2016, absent congressional action. However, because the provisions governing orders under civilian agency contracts are codified in a different section of the United States Code than those governing orders under defense agency contracts, it is possible that differences in the treatment of civilian and defense agency orders could again arise if Congress were to amend Title 10 without amending Title 41, or vice versa.

## End Notes

[1] National Defense Authorization Act for FY2012, P.L. 112-81, §813,—Stat.—(Dec. 31, 2011).

[2] In so finding, GAO, in particular, assumed, without deciding, that the identity of the agency that awarded the underlying contract, and not that of the agency issuing the challenged order, determines whether the protest is governed by the provisions in Title 10 of the United States Code or those in Title 41 of the United States Code. *See* Technatomy Corp., B-405130, at 2 n.1 (June 14, 2011). The provisions of Title 10 generally apply to the procurements of defense agencies, while the provisions of Title 41 generally apply to the procurements of civilian agencies.

[3] Like the cases upon which it is based, the discussion of orders in this report excludes orders issued under the Federal Supply Schedules (FSS). While FSS contracts can be characterized as task and delivery order contracts, GAO and the courts historically found that orders under FSS contracts were protestable, notwithstanding the Federal Acquisition Streamlining Act (FASA) and the National Defense Authorization Act (NDAA) for Fiscal Year 2008, because their issuance is governed by a different section of the Federal Acquisition Regulation (FAR) than that governing orders under non-FSS contracts. *See, e.g.*, Labat-Anderson, Inc. v. United States, 50 Fed. Cl. 99, 104 (2001). However, it should be noted that, although the *Technatomy* protest involved an FSS contract, GAO did not address its possible jurisdiction in light of *Labat-Anderson* and related cases.

[4] *See, e.g.*, Mason Alinger, Recent Developments in Task and Delivery Order Contracting, 39 *Pub. Cont. L. J.* 839, 839 (2010) (stating that the NDAA for FY2008 "temporarily expanded [GAO's] jurisdiction to consider protests regarding certain task and delivery orders"); Ryan Roberts, Does Automatic Mean Automatic? The Applicability of the CICA Automatic Stay to Task and Delivery Order Bid Protests, 39 *Pub. Cont. L.J.* 641, 652 n.79 (2010) (suggesting that the inclusion of the sunset provision "demonstrate[s] legislative skepticism as to the benefit of task and delivery order protests, and therefore the new jurisdiction will either be a short-lived anomaly or a test run for later permanent jurisdiction").

[5] Procuring agencies had construed the 2008 amendments to FASA to mean that they lacked jurisdiction over protests regarding the issuance of orders valued in excess of $10 million. *See, e.g.*, Memorandum from Al Matera, Chairman, Civilian Agency Acquisition Council, Office of the Chief Acquisition Officer, Gen. Servs. Admin., to Civilian Agencies Other than NASA, Enhanced Competition for Task and Delivery Order Contracts, May 23, 2008 (copy on file with the authors). However, agencies could potentially have found that they had such jurisdiction under the reasoning adopted by GAO and the Court of Federal Claims.

[6] P.L. 103-355, 108 Stat. 3243 (1994).

[7] P.L. 110-181, §843, 122 Stat. 236-39 (Oct. 14, 2008).

[8] P.L. 111-383, §825, 124 Stat. 4270 (Jan. 7, 2011).

[9] *See, e.g.*, James K. Nagle, *History of Government Contracting* 506-07 (2d ed. 1999) (describing such aspects of preFASA procurements as specifications for sugar cookies that were 15 pages long; bid documents weighing three tons; and soldiers during the Gulf War requesting their families to send them commercial global positioning systems that reportedly worked better than the Army's navigational gear).

10 A&D Fire Protection Inc. v. United States, 72 Fed. Cl. 126, 133 (2006) (internal quotations omitted) (quoting 140 *Cong. Rec.* H9240 (1994) (statement of Rep. Conyers). *See also* Recent Developments in Task and Delivery Order Contracting, *supra* note 4, at 839. Congress further streamlined aspects of federal procurement when it enacted the Federal Acquisition Reform Act (FARA) of 1996 (P.L. 104-106, div. D) and the Services Acquisition Reform Act (SARA) of 2003 (P.L. 108-136, tit. XIV).

[11] *See* P.L. 103-355, §1004, 108 Stat. 3249-50 (codified at 10 USC. §2304a(a)) (procurements of defense agencies); *id.*, §1054, 108 Stat. 3261 (codified at 41 USC. §4103(a)) (procurements of civilian agencies). Although they lacked explicit statutory authority to do so, agencies used task and delivery order (TO/DO) contracts prior to 1994, and some commentators had asserted that TO/DO contracts were sometimes "improper[ly] use[d] ... to avoid competing new or expanded requirements when competition is appropriate, or ensure proper approval of the justification when it is not." *See Report of the Advisory Panel on Streamlining and Codifying Acquisition Laws*, quoted in John Cibinic, Jr., Task and Delivery Order Contracting: Great Concept, Poor Implementation, 12 *Nash & Cibinic Rep.* 30, May 1998, at 75- 76. For this reason, the Advisory Panel (also known as the "Section 800 Panel") recommended the codification of TO/DO contract authority, a recommendation which Congress adopted when it enacted FASA.

[12] 48 C.F.R. §16.501-1.

[13] *See* 48 C.F.R. §16.501-2(a).

[14] Multiple-award task order contracts are sometimes also referred to as MATOCs. Only firms holding the underlying contract may generally compete for orders issued under the contract.

[15] The Administrative Procedure Act (APA) generally furnishes the substantive standard used in determining whether agency conduct in the award or proposed award of a government contract is permissible. *See* 5 USC. §706(2)(A) (scope of review under the APA); Superior Helicopter LLC v. United States, 78 Fed. Cl. 181, 186-87 (2007) (application of APA to agency procurement activities).

[16] *See, e.g.*, Nautica Int'l, Inc., B-254428 (Dec. 15, 1993); Data Comm'ns Sys. Corp., B-227340 (Aug. 6, 1987).

[17] *See* P.L. 103-355, §1004, 108 Stat. 3252 (codified at 10 USC. §2304c(a)(1)) ("The following actions are not required for issuance of a task or delivery order under a task or delivery order contract: ... a competition (or [an approved] waiver of competition...) that is separate from that used for entering into the contract."); *id.* at §1054, 198 Stat. 3264 (codified at 41

USC. §4106(b)(2)) (same). However, FASA did establish a general preference for multiple-award contracts and generally requires agencies to give all contractors holding the contract "a fair opportunity to be considered" for each order valued in excess of $3,000. *Id.*, §1004, 108 Stat. 3250-52 (codified at 10 USC. §2304a(d); 10 USC. §2304c(b)); *id.*, at §1054, 108 Stat. 3262-64 (codified at 41 USC. §4103(d)(4); 41 USC. §4106(c)). Congress subsequently enacted legislation requiring that the FAR be amended to provide "specific guidance" on the appropriate use of multiple-award TO/DO contracts, as well as the steps that agencies should take to ensure that contractors have a "fair opportunity to be considered" for orders. *See* NDAA for FY2000, P.L. 106-65, §804, 113 Stat. 704 (Oct. 5, 1999). It also required that "smaller" orders (i.e., those valued in excess of the simplified acquisition threshold (generally $150,000) but below $5 million) issued under defense contracts be awarded on a "competitive basis," which means that (1) "fair notice" of the intent to make the purchase is provided to all contractors offering that good or service under the contract, and (2) all contractors responding to the notice are afforded a "fair opportunity" to make an offer and have that offer considered by the official making the purchase. NDAA for FY2002, P.L. 107-107, §803, 115 Stat. 1178-79 (Dec. 28, 2001). Similar later requirements were later imposed on "smaller" orders under civilian agency contracts. *See infra* note 26.

[18] *See, e.g.*, *Federal Acquisition Trends, Reforms and Challenges: Hearings before the Subcomm. on Gov't Mgmt., Info. & Tech. of the H. Comm. on Gov't Reform, 106th Cong.*, 6-7 (2000) (statement of Henry L. Hinton, Jr., Assistant Comptroller General).

[19] *See, e.g.*, S. REP. NO. 103-259, at 7 (FASA "revise[d] and simplif[ied] the bid protest process with a view towards reducing the number of protest that are filed"); James Fontana, Multiple Awards: A Protest-Proof Process, 13 *Wash. Tech.* 18 (Dec. 10, 1998) (characterizing use of TO/DO contracts under FASA as "virtually protest-proof").

[20] P.L. 103-355, §1004, 108 Stat. 3253 (codified, as amended, at 10 USC. §2304c(e)); *id.* at §1054, 108 Stat. 3261 (codified, as amended, at 41 USC. §4106(f)). In an attempt to provide contractors with additional opportunities to challenge alleged agency misconduct in the issuance of orders, FASA also directed all executive agencies using TO/DO contracts to appoint a task and delivery order ombudsman, who "shall be responsible for reviewing complaints from the contractors on such contracts and ensuring that all of the contractors are afforded a fair opportunity to be considered" for certain orders. *Id.*, §1004, 108 Stat. 3253 (codified at 10 USC. §2304c(f)); *id.*, at §1054, 108 Stat. 3254 (codified at 41 USC. §4106(g)).

[21] *See, e.g.*, Does Automatic Mean Automatic?, *supra* note 4, at 642.

[22] *See, e.g.*, Ralph C. Nash, Jr. & John Cibinic, Jr., Taming the Task Order Contract: Congress Tries Again, 22 *Nash & Cibinic Rep.* 31 (May 2008), at 75 (noting instances of improper use of TO/DO contracts, including "broad contract scopes, 10-year ordering periods, poorly defined task orders with long performance periods, options to extend task order performance for years on end, and open-ended hourly-rate-based pricing schemes that defy meaningful comparative evaluation during source selection"); Michael C. Wong, Current Problems with Multiple Award Indefinite Delivery/Indefinite Quantity Contracts: A Primer, *The Army Lawyer*, Sept. 2006, at 25, 27 (same).

[23] *See, e.g.*, *Labat-Anderson*, 50 Fed. Cl. at 104 (protest of order under FSS contract not barred by FASA because the order was issued under Part 8 of the FAR, not Part 16); Electro-Voice, Inc., B-278319; B-278319.2 (Jan. 15, 1998) (finding that FASA's bar on protests of orders that do not increase the scope, period, or maximum value of the underlying contract does not apply to "downselections," or two-step procurement processes wherein the number of

potential competitors is first reduced by preliminary screening and then a competition is conducted among the remaining firms); L-3 Comm'ns Corp., ASBCA No. 54920, 06-2 B.C.A. (CCH) 33,374, at 165,451 (noting that breach of the contract clause obligating agencies to give contractors a "fair opportunity to be considered" "may theoretically be grounds for both a 'protest' seeking to cancel or modify the award and a 'claim' for damages").

[24] *Report of the Acquisition Advisory Panel to the Office of Federal Procurement Policy and the United States Congress* 108 (2007) (recommending that contractors be authorized to protest orders valued in excess of $5 million that do not increase the scope, period, or maximum value of the underlying contract). Industry groups and the Office of Federal Procurement Policy generally opposed authorizing such protests. *See, e.g.*, James J. McCullough, Acquisition Reform Revisited: Section 843 Protests Against Task and Delivery Orders at GAO, 50 *Gov't Cont.* 75, Mar. 5, 2008, at 1; Office of Mgmt. & Budget, Statement of Administration Policy on S. 1547, National Defense Authorization Act for FY2008, at 5 (July 10, 2007) (copy on file with authors) (expressing concern that authorizing protests of "large" orders could delay the procurement process).

[25] P.L. 110-181, §843(a), 122 Stat. 236-37 (codified at 10 USC. §2304a(d)(3)(A)); *id.*, at §843(b), 122 Stat. 238-39 (codified at 41 USC. §4103(d)(3)(A)). Single-award TO/DO contracts valued in excess of $100 million may be used only when the agency head determines in writing that (1) the task or delivery orders expected under the contract are so integrally related that only a single source can reasonably perform the work; (2) the contract provides for only firm fixed price task or delivery orders for products for which unit prices are established in the contract, or services for which prices are established in the contract for the specific tasks to be performed; (3) only one source is qualified and capable of performing the work at a reasonable price to the government; and (4) because of exceptional circumstances, it is necessary in the public interest to award the contract to a single source.

[26] *Id.*, at §843(a)(2), 122 Stat. 237 (codified at 10 USC. §2304c(d)); *id.*, at §843(b)(2), 122 Stat. 238-39 (codified at 41 USC. §4106(d)). Under the 2008 amendments, contractors have not had a "fair opportunity to be considered" unless they are provided with (1) a notice of the task or delivery order that includes a clear statement of the agency's requirements; (2) a reasonable period of time to provide a proposal in response to the notice; (3) disclosure of the significant factors and subfactors that the agency expects to consider in evaluating the proposals and their relative importance; (4) in the case of an award that is made on the basis of "best value," a written statement documenting the basis for the award and the relative importance of quality and price or cost factors; and (5) the opportunity for a post-award debriefing. The 110th Congress later expanded the competition requirements for TO/DO contracts of civilian agencies when it enacted the Duncan Hunter NDAA for FY2009. Among other things, this act requires that orders valued in excess of the simplified acquisition threshold (generally $150,000) and below $5 million be issued on a "competitive basis" unless certain conditions are met. P.L. 110-417, §863, 122 Stat. 4547 (Oct. 14, 2008). In addition, the 2009 act also generally requires that notices related to sole-source task and delivery issues be posted on FedBizOpps (https://www.fbo.gov/) within 14 days of being placed. *Id.*, §863(c), 122 Stat. 4547-48.

[27] P.L. 110-181, §843(a)(2), 122 Stat. 237 (codified, as amended, at 10 USC. §2304c(e)(1)); *id.*, at §843(b)(2), 122 Stat. 239 (codified at 41 USC. §4106(f)(1)). The Senate version of the NDAA for FY2008 would have authorized protests of orders valued in excess of $5 million. However, the House version, which authorized protests of orders valued in excess of $10 million, prevailed in conference. *See* H.R. REP. NO. 110-417, at 956 (2007).

[28] P.L. 110-181, §843(a)(2), 122 Stat. 237 (codified, as amended, at 10 USC. §2304c(e)(2)); *id.*, at §843(b)(2), 122 Stat. 239 (codified at 41 USC. §4106(f)(2)).

[29] *Id.*, at §843(a)(2), 122 Stat. 237 (codified, as amended, at 10 USC. §2304c(e)(3)); *id.*, at §843(b)(2), 122 Stat. 239 (codified at 41 USC. §4106(f)(3)).

[30] *See supra* note 4 and accompanying text.

[31] *See* H.R. REP. NO. 110-477, at 956 (2007) ("The conferees expect that the sunset date will provide Congress with an opportunity to review implementation of the provision and make any necessary adjustments.").

[32] *See* Technatomy Corp., B-405130, at 2.

[33] P.L. 111-383, §825, 124 Stat. 4270 (Jan. 7, 2011) (codified at 10 USC. §2304c(e)) (emphasis added).

[34] 41 USC. §4106(f) (emphasis added).

[35] GAO assumed, and the parties did not contest, that the order in question did not expand the scope, period, or maximum value of the underlying contract. *See* Technatomy Corp., B-405130, at 2 n.1. Because GAO is a legislative branch agency, the "separation of powers" doctrine means that its recommendations are not legally binding upon executive branch agencies. *See* Ameron, Inc. v. United States Army Corps of Eng'rs, 809 F.2d 979, 987 (3d Cir. 1986) ("The doctrine of separation of powers gives each branch of the government constitutional rights. These rights are of tremendous importance, as they insure that our government functions properly. They thereby serve as bulwarks to the freedom which the doctrine of separation of powers is intended to preserve."). Thus, the executive branch may—and, in fact, recently has—construed statutes in ways that contradict GAO's recommendations. *See* CRS Report R40591, *Set-Asides for Small Businesses: Recent Developments in the Law Regarding Precedence Among the Set-Aside Programs and Set-Asides Under Indefinite-Delivery/Indefinite-Quantity Contracts*, by Kate M. Manuel (discussing disagreements in 2008-2010 between GAO and the executive branch as to whether set-asides for Historically Underutilized Business Zone (HUBZone) small businesses had "precedence" over set-asides for other small businesses under the Small Business Act). Agencies are, however, required by statute to notify GAO when they do not "fully adopt" any recommendations made by GAO in a bid protest. 31 USC. §3554(b)(3). GAO, in turn, is then required to notify four separate congressional committees: the Senate Committee on Homeland Security and Governmental Affairs, the Senate Committee on Appropriations, the House Committee on Oversight and Government Reform, and the House Committee on Appropriations. 31 USC. §3554(e)(1)(A)-(B).

[36] Technatomy Corp., B-405130, at 2 n.1. GAO agreed with DOD's argument that the law governing protests of orders issued by civilian agencies should apply here because the order in question was issued under a multiple-award contract awarded by GSA. *Id.* at 2 n.1. However, it rejected DOD's argument that the decision should be based upon the law in effect at the time when the protest was heard, as opposed to the time when the protest was filed. *Id.* at 12- 14.

[37] *Id.* at 8 ("Where, as here, the language of a statute is clear on its face, its plain meaning will be given effect.") (citing Carcieri v. Salazar, 555 US 379, 129 S. Ct. 1058, 1063-64 (2009)).

[38] *Id.* at 9.

[39] *Id.* at 8-9.

[40] *Id.* at 7. In addition to establishing the competition requirements for federal contracts, CICA expressly authorized GAO to hear bid protests. However, GAO had heard protests prior to CICA on the theory that its authority to settle and adjust "all claims and demands" against

the United States encompassed bid protests. *See* CRS Report R40228, *GAO Bid Protests: An Overview of Time Frames and Procedures*, by Kate M. Manuel and Moshe Schwartz.

[41] B-405130, at 10.

[42] Previously, the court had found that GAO had exclusive jurisdiction over such protests because of the amendments made to FASA by the NDAA for FY2008. *See, e.g.*, DataMill, Inc. v. United States, 91 Fed. Cl. 740 (Mar. 5, 2010).

[43] 2011 US Claims LEXIS 1872, at *14 (Aug. 19, 2011).

[44] *Id.* at *14-*15.

[45] *Id.* at *14.

[46] *Id.* at *15. According to the court, "[t]he proposed legislation demonstrates two things. First, the perceived need for it suggests that Congress understands that the existing sunset provision does not accomplish the same result. Second, the proposals demonstrate that Congress can legislate with precision when it chooses to do so. Both observations reinforce our reluctance to follow the government's invitation to tell Congress what we think it really intended in 2008."). *Id.*

[47] *Cf.* Daniel J. Kelly, David Himelfarb, and Bonnie A. Vanzler, GAO Opens the Door to Protests of All Civilian Agency Task Orders ... But for How Long?, 96 *Fed. Cont. Rep.* 259 (Sept. 13, 2011) (suggesting that GAO's decision "opens the floodgates to many protests that were previously barred"). Specifically, under the GAO and Court of Federal Claims decisions, protesters would have had greater opportunities to protest the issuance of orders under civilian agency contracts than under defense agency contracts, particularly after September 30, 2016. When civilian agency contracts were involved, contractors would have been able to challenge orders of any size (regardless of whether these orders increase the scope, period, or maximum value of the contract) before GAO, the Court of Federal Claims, and, potentially, the procuring agencies. However, when defense contracts were involved, contractors would have been able to challenge "large" orders that do not increase the scope, period, or maximum value of the contract only before GAO. Moreover, absent congressional action, GAO's jurisdiction over "large" defense orders would have expired on September 30, 2016, and contractors would have been able to challenge only defense orders that increased the scope, period, or maximum value of the contract under which they are issued after September 30, 2016.

[48] A 2009 report indicated that GAO's expanded jurisdiction over protests of "large" orders "has caused few problems and resulted in only a small increase in the number of cases sent to [GAO] for adjudication." David Hubler, New Rule on Task-Order Protests Not Causing Problems, Panel Says, *Wash. Tech.*, Dec. 14, 2009, *available at* http://washington technology.com/Articles/2009/12/14/New-task-order-law-causes-few-problems-panel-says.aspx. However, the number of protests of "large" orders heard by GAO has increased every year since 2009, and the report was issued at a time when GAO could only hear protests of "large" orders, not all orders, issued under civilian agency contracts. *See* GAO Bid Protest Annual Report to Congress for Fiscal Year 2010, Nov. 23, 2010, *available at* http://www.gao.gov/special.pubs/bidpro10.pdf (noting that 189 of the 2,299 protest filed with GAO in FY2010 were due to its expanded jurisdiction over protests of large orders); GAO Bid Protest Annual Report to Congress for Fiscal Year 2009, Jan. 8, 2010, *available at* http://www.gao.gov/special.pubs/bidpro09.pdf (noting that 139 of the 1,989 protest filed with GAO in FY2009 were due to its expanded jurisdiction over protests of large orders); GAO Bid Protest Annual Report to Congress for Fiscal Year 2008, Dec. 22, 2008, *available at* http://www.gao.gov/special.pubs/ bidpro08.pdf (noting that 49 of the 1,652 protest filed with GAO in FY2008 were due to its expanded jurisdiction over protests of large orders).

[49] Dep't of Defense, Gen. Servs. Admin., Nat'l Aeronautics & Space Admin., Federal Acquisition Regulation: Extension of Sunset Date for Protests of Task and Delivery Orders, 76 Fed. Reg. 39238 (July 5, 2011) (codified at 48 C.F.R. §16.505(a)(9)) (emphasis added).

[50] *See supra* note 35.

[51] In particular, the FAR's reference to "subpart" would appear to encompass protests on both grounds.

[52] 467 US 837 (1984).

[53] *Id.* at 412. *See, e.g.*, Mission Critical Solutions v. United States, 91 Fed. Cl. 386 (2010) (finding that Small Business Administration regulations providing for "parity" among the set-aside programs was not entitled to deference under *Chevron* because it did not constitute a reasonable interpretation of the Small Business Act).

[54] P.L. 112-81, §813,—Stat.—(Dec. 31, 2011) (to be codified at 41 USC. §4106(f)).

# INDEX

## C

## F



## G

## H



## I



## J



## K

## L



## M



## N

## O



## P



## Q



## R

## S

## W